The Complete Book
of Offensive Line Play

THE COMPLETE BOOK
OF
OFFENSIVE LINE PLAY

Nick Metrokotsas

Parker Publishing Company, Inc.

West Nyack, New York

©1977, *by*

PARKER PUBLISHING COMPANY, INC.

West Nyack, N.Y.

Library of Congress Cataloging in Publication Data

Metrokotsas, Nick,
   The complete book of offensive line play.

   Includes index.
   1. Football--Offense. I. Title.
GV951.8.M47   796.33'223   76-41230
ISBN 0-13-157545-7

To the late Ernie Jorge, Head Offensive Line Coach, U.S. Naval Academy, 1955-1966, for his inspiration, enthusiasm, and wit, and to all the men who are associated with the great game of football.

Nick Metrokotsas

What This Book
Offers the Coach

HOW TO BLOCK FOR THE RUNNING GAME

In the first three chapters of the book, over sixty illustrations are used to explain the fundamentals of one-on-one blocking styles, combination blocks, such as cross-blocks and double-team blocks, and trap blocks. This first section concludes with a description of some individual blocking styles that the coach may want to teach to special players, either by virtue of their position, or because of the player's physical size and qualifications.

HOW TO BLOCK MULTIPLE DEFENSES

In the introductory chapter to this topic, the reader will find analyses of various defenses that a football team may encounter throughout the course of a season. The purposes and uses of those defenses are explained with emphasis on their effect on the running game. Chapter 5 explains how to establish simple and consistent rule blocking, a system that will accommodate multiple defensive opponents. Finally, the reader is provided with a system with which the type of block may be "called" by the players involved with the blocking at the point of attack. In closing, there appears an explanation of the advantages of this "call system" of offensive blocking.

HOW TO BLOCK FOR THE PASSING GAME

Here the reader finds techniques for teaching the simplest and most consistent system for pass protection. The drop-back pass, the sprint-out pass, and the play action pass are featured styles of the passing game in these chapters. Also offered is a bit of our own philosophy on the importance and the advantages of a sound passing game.

HOW TO BLOCK FOR ALL PHASES OF THE KICKING GAME

Everyone realizes the importance of the punt and the kick-off return, but how many coaches are prepared to give the kick-off, the quick-kick or the extra point equal consideration. These chapters offer suggestions that will make the complete kicking game an effective offensive weapon with an emphasis on organization. Several very good return patterns for punts and kick-offs, are suggested. These blocking techniques are tied in with those given in the previous chapters. These chapters show how to simplify the teaching of blocking techniques for all phases of offensive line play.

HOW TO HELP YOUR LINEMEN PREPARE PHYSICALLY

These last chapters help the reader with methods he can use to prepare his players physically for the rigors of football. Some of the highlights in this section include a chapter on weight-training methods especially for the offensive lineman, exercises and drills that help increase speed and quickness and some helpful hints that may reduce the number of injuries sustained by the athlete in the vital areas of the legs and upper body. In all, this section provides the reader with an out-of-season conditioning program that will make the in-season coaching more rewarding for a group of healthy athletes.

N.M.

Table of Contents

The Complete Book
of Offensive Line Play

part I

How to Block
for the Running Game

chapter 1

One-on-One Blocking

Since this book teaches all phases of offensive line play, we feel that it is necessary to introduce it with a statement of our coaching philosophy in this area. Simply stated, our philosophy is: "A great block begins with a great stance." It is difficult to imagine how a great block, which depends on quickness, balance, visibility and power, could ever be executed from a stance that did not lend itself to these characteristics. Therefore, we spend a great deal of time with our linemen in order to develop a stance that will permit them to execute their blocking assignments with maximum quickness, perfect balance, 100 percent visibility and tremendous power.

THE PERFECT STANCE

QUICKNESS

In order to insure quickness, three techniques are important. The first and most important is proper weight distribution. The lineman who sits back on his feet can not hope to move quickly straight ahead. Offensive linemen are often called on to pull to either side, fire-out straight, step left or right and set up in pass protection. In any assignment, the blocker must be set in the same stance, a stance that will allow him to move in all directions with maximum effectiveness. It is up to the coach to help his blockers find such a stance. This can be done by encouraging these techniques:

1. The heels of the feet should be raised off the ground slightly, putting weight slightly forward.
2. The coach can check weight distribution by looking at the blocker's profile and making certain that the tail is slightly higher than the head.

BALANCE

The next important part of a great stance is balance. Since balance is vital in the actual execution of the block, the coach should consider it equally as vital to the stance. For most players, balance is synonymous with "comfort." If the stance is comfortable it may also be balanced, but the coach should check the position of the feet for perfection of the stance. Line play is varied in what it entails, and many times a blocker will be hit from the side when he least expects it. It is therefore necessary for him to assume a wider stance than any other player. The proper width of the stance will vary with the player's weight, but generally it can be described as slightly wider than shoulder width. In the interest of comfort, many players will stagger one foot. The right-handed player will put his right hand down on the ground and drop his right foot back. The left-hander will do just the opposite. A proper guage of this stagger distance would be heel-to-toe as a rule. (See Diagram 1-1.)

Right-Handed Blocker   Left-Handed Player

Diagram 1-1

VISIBILITY

When we refer to visibility in blocking, we are actually saying that you can't block what you can't see! The perfect stance should allow the blocker to see the defenders immediately in front of him, regardless of whether they are defensive linemen or linebackers.

The blocker must also be able to see defenders in either gap, for these are all the people that he would have to be responsible for blocking on a given play directed in his area. In order to insure this visibility, the blocker should not choose a stance that forces his head to look toward the ground. He must try to get as much height out of his stance as possible. This can be accomplished in part by using a two-point stance. This stance is used almost exclusively in the kicking game; however, it does not allow the blocker maximum quickness straight ahead. A four-point stance is also popular with coaches who emphasize straight ahead, one-on-one blocking, but here again a blocker is at a disadvantage when trying to pull out of the line. So much of his weight is distributed and spread out, that pulling to trap or lead end-runs is difficult. The stance that we feel allows for maximum visibility, without denying the blocker the use of any of his techniques, is the three-point stance. Therefore, throughout this book, we will advocate the use of the three-point stance with all blocking types discussed. As a final extra technique which makes the stance even more conducive to the types of blocks in our system, we have the blockers put their fingertips on the ground instead of the knuckles. This gives them an extra bit of height and a more flexible surface from which they can push off on pulling assignments.

POWER

The final element of the perfect block is power. Power is a form of potential energy in this case, for once the three-point stance has been perfected, the potential for power exists; otherwise, a successful, powerful block is just a case of luck. The complete description of the perfect three-point stance is as follows:

1. Feet slightly wider than shoulder width.
2. Toe of back foot even with heel of "up" foot.
3. Fingertips, not knuckles, on the ground.
4. Heels raised off the ground.
5. Tail end higher than head, with head up.

SPLITS IN THE LINE

The size of the split between linemen should be guided by the nature of each play. We believe in flexible rules for splits, and they are incorporated in each and every play. By doing this, the size of the split changes with the play and actually becomes part of our stance. This means that when we coach the proper stance, we are also demanding that the player know his split rules. In this way we not only get the blocker in the proper stance for each play, but we also have the exact split we want. The split changes in size as the play changes and is guided by the following rules:

1. If the play calls for a power block, such as a double-team, then the split between the two blockers will be tighter.

2. If the play calls for a cross block or an influence block, then the splits will be wider.

3. If the play is being run to the far side of any lineman, we have the lineman split wider to force the defender to split with him. This helps keep the defender farther away from the play.

4. If the play is being run to the same side of the lineman, then we ask him to tighten his split in order to keep the defender inside in a position where he can be hooked and prevented from pursuing to the outside.

The main point here is that when we stress the word "stance," we include the concept of splits between linemen with these guidelines in mind. The whole purpose of teaching proper line splits is to get the best angle on the defender in order to keep him far from the point of attack. Although many coaches may not employ this technique in the interior of their line, almost every coach uses a variation in the split of his receivers in order to alter defensive setups. A typical example is of course, the flex split used by the tight end when he is going to receive a pass as opposed to his tighter split when he is going to double-team with the tackle.

Throughout the course of the book, when we speak of proper stance, we also imply the technique of proper splits.

THE THREE COMMANDMENTS OF BLOCKING

All blocking is predicated on three basic commandments. In order they are:

1. *Quick start off the line of scrimmage.* The quicker off the ball a lineman is, the better are his chances of overcoming the defender's use of hands. Other defensive weapons such as slants, blitzes, forearm shivers and "reading" can be made ineffective by a quick charge.

2. *Good initial contact.* It is imperative that proper contact be

made by the blocker to insure that he will be using the greatest surface area of his body to stop the defender's charge and ultimately move him out of the play. Depending on the defender's alignment and the block type being used, the surface of contact will vary from the blocker's shoulder to his hip.

3. *Acceleration on contact.* Once contact has been made, the blocker's next objective is to move the defender out of position. All too often the blocker concentrates his maximum efforts on quickness and initial contact, but falls to his knees because he did not accelerate his feet on contact. This is the most important aspect of all, for without it no block is truly a great one. Yet, if a blocker is too slow getting off the ball, or if he makes poor initial contact, he can still make a successful block by accelerating his feet when he does make contact. Many sports demand this technique also, only the word most commonly used to describe what we want here is "follow-through." In football, the term accelerate has more meaning since it demands that the blocker actually run faster.

There are many types of blocks that the offensive lineman can use to move a defender from any defensive alignment. In all situations the variables have nothing to do with the fundamentals of line play. The blocker must *always* have a perfect stance, he must *always* fire-out quickly off the ball, he must *always* make good initial contact, and he must *always* accelerate the feet on contact. The only adjustments may be the part of the body used to make contact with the defender or the steps taken to get to him, and these will be discussed in detail throughout the book. Adjusting the blocking surface is a technique that can be coached and, in many cases, used by the individual lineman at his own discretion. The first such technique is the scramble block.

THE SCRAMBLE BLOCK

The term "scramble" means that the blocker must fire-out from his three-point stance and go into a four-point crawl position. As we mentioned earlier, the four-point stance is very effective against one-on-one blocking situations, so we teach this technique for those linemen faced with a defender playing head on. Contact is made by the blocker at the defender's mid-section and thigh area. If the contact is made properly, the blocker will have already accomplished two important things:

1. He will have avoided the defender's forearm or hand-shiver.
2. He will have nullified any advantage the defender had in weight or strength.

The blocker is using all his strength and power to move the defender, but the defender's strength has been avoided. Furthermore, by attacking the defender in this way, the blocker stifles the defender's ability to pursue or use his legs.

The scramble block is not complete until the blocker has turned the defender down the line of scrimmage away from the point of attack. Using his hands on the ground and moving in a crab-like fashion makes this job relatively easy once proper contact is made. Acceleration after contact is the secret to mainting contact after the scramble position is attained. This block type is not effective against a stand-up defender such as a linebacker or a defensive end, because it would be easy for them to back up and avoid contact. In order to drill for the scramble block, we advocate the use of two special drills, the "board" drill and the "nutcracker" drill:

> 1. *The board drill.* Using a wooden 2" x 8" plank with beveled edges, the coach will place a blocker at one end and a defender directly in front of him in the down position. On the coach's command, the defender will catch the blocker as he fires-out and provide him with resistance. This drill teaches the blocker to fire-out quickly, make good contact, and accelerate his feet on contact in order to move the defender down the length of the plank. (See Diagrams 1-2 through 1-4).

The Board Drill

Diagram 1-2: Start.   Diagram 1-3: Contact.   Diagram 1-4: Acceleration.

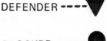
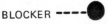

a. *Start.* Check stance of the blocker. Put defender head-on in three or four-point stance. (Diagram 1-2.)

   b. *Contact.* The blocker gets his head and shoulders under the groin area of the defender. The head is up, feet apart, and the blocker begins to "crab." (Diagram 1-3.)

   c. *Acceleration.* The blocker now accelerates his feet and does not stop until the defender is driven to the end of the board. This also encourages the blocker to maintain contact for a long duration. (Diagram 1-4.)

2. *The nutcracker drill.* Put a blocker and a defender in the same starting position as in the board drill, only now create a simulated hole by placing them between two dummies lying down on the ground. On the coach's count, the blocker fires-out and uses a scramble block to move the defender out of the alley between the dummies. A ball carrier is generally added to this drill so that he can read the block and make his cut properly. The blocker is instructed to take the defender in any direction he can, usually in the direction the defender wants to go. (See Diagram 1-5.)

The Nutcracker Drill

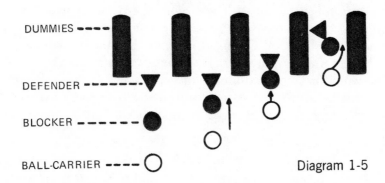

DUMMIES

DEFENDER

BLOCKER

BALL-CARRIER   Diagram 1-5

THE DRIVE BLOCK

Many coaches refer to this type of block as the "bull" block, but regardless of the terminology used, the connotation is the same. In this type of one-on-one block, the linemen use their eyes as an aiming device in order to keep sight of their target. The proper execution of the block is accomplished when the blocker slides his head to one side and drives his shoulder into the defender and, at the same time, brings his fists or forearms up into the defender's body. Most coaches are wary of teaching the drive block for fear that their players will sustain injuries to their necks. Since the actual blocking surface is the shoulder, fists or forearms and chest, only improper coaching and/or execution of this technique will result in injury. But this is a fact that applies to all phases of football, whether it is running the ball, getting tackled, making tackles or executing various blocks. The complete technique must be mastered and then put to use properly.

TECHNIQUES OF THE DRIVE BLOCK

1. Start with a perfect stance.
2. Make good initial contact with the shoulder, forearms, and fists.
3. The block is complete when the blocker begins to accelerate and rise up to use his chest on the defender.

The drive block is used for blocking defenders in any position. The reasons for its use are many. First, let's suppose you are facing a defense that slants on the snap of the ball. The defender will line up in a head-on position, but, on the snap of the ball, he takes an angle step one way or another into the gap on one side of the blocker. If the blocker is quick off the ball and aims at his target with his eyes, making good initial contact, the slanting defender can be picked up on the blocker's shoulder. On the other hand, had the blocker aimed his shoulder at the defender as the surface of contact, the slanting technique would have caused him to miss the block entirely. It must be understood that contact is not to be made with the head, but this point of reference should serve as an aiming device in all our blocking.

1. Begin every drill with a perfect stance.
2. The proper initial step is taken and the head is up using the eyes as an aiming device.
3. Using the eyes as an aiming device enables the blocker to see the slanting action and get in front of the defender.
4. The block is complete when the blocker accelerates.

RISE-UP AND ACCELERATE

As we progress from the scramble block to the drive block, we add a technique called "rising up." We ask that our blockers try to arch their backs as they accelerate in an effort to stand up and run over the defender. This rising action makes the job of accelerating easier, and helps to get our blockers to carry out their blocks for a longer period of time. Furthermore, it enables the blocker to react to the tough defender who backs up and spins out. Rising-up can be drilled at half speed against airshields and at full speed against a defender in a one-on-one situation. Since a certain amount of strength is required in order to execute this technique properly, we use the two-man sled or the seven-man sled to drill the rising-up action necessary in the drive block. The instructions below tell how this drill can be run.

Drilling for Rising-Up

1. The blockers take their stances directly in front of the sled pads and apply steady pressure to the machine. The coach encourages good body position in this phase.

2. On a command by the coach, the blockers must arch their backs and rise-up on the sled. They can immediately begin to accelerate their feet and drive the sled. On the coach's command they actually explode into the sled driving their fists or forearms into the pads.

THE NEAR SHOULDER BLOCK

This is perhaps the most common block used by offensive linemen. It is called near shoulder, because the blocker will use the shoulder *nearest* the defender to make initial contact. If the defender is on the blocker's left, he will make contact with the left shoulder, and vice versa. It is most effective when used against the defender who does not slant away from the blocker, but plays a more or less normal reading technique.

The near shoulder block is designed to move the defender down the line of scrimmage and away from the immediate point of attack. It is not very useful in preventing the defender from penetrating through the line of scrimmage. Practical uses for the near shoulder block would be:

1. Double-team blocking.
2. Trap blocking.
3. One-on-one blocking on dive plays.
4. Quick openers.
5. Option plays.
6. Blocking for the "veer" offense.

Very seldom is the defender in a head-on position. One reason being that this position gives neither the blocker nor the defender an advantage, unless of course the two linemen are mismatched in size and strength. Therefore, blockers are confronted with defenders who are in gaps to either side of them, stand-up defenders who play farther away from them, and even some defenders who play halfway on and halfway off one shoulder. (See Diagrams 1-6 through 1-9.)

Varying Defensive Alignments

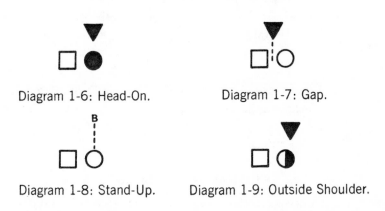

Diagram 1-6: Head-On.   Diagram 1-7: Gap.

Diagram 1-8: Stand-Up.   Diagram 1-9: Outside Shoulder.

THE STEP DRILL

It therefore becomes vital that the initial step taken by the blocker gets him to the defender as quickly as possible through the shortest route. We teach our linemen to step directly towards the defender with the foot nearest the defender. Thus, if the defender we want to block is on our right side, we step with the right foot directly towards him on the initial step. That first step is vital to the entire block, for it puts the blocker in a good position to make a square, well-balanced block as quickly as possible. The blocker must remember this step technique for each and every block he uses, and we stress it's importance with a simple axiom: "If you are to block to your right, then step to the right with your right foot, and if you are to block to your left, step to the left with your left foot." This simple but all-important technique is underemphasized by many coaches, and yet it should become a major part of your daily practice routine.

A very simple drill that we use called step drill can accomplish wonders in getting the blocker to make the correct initial step every time. A group of blockers are lined up in columns and rows facing their coach. From their proper stance, the blockers take one step in the direction specified by the coach's command. This drill also teaches unity in movement, and the coach can readily see which linemen are quicker than others. During the drill the coach must demand quickness and proper body balance. Since the step drill is a group drill, specific steps can be coached at the same time. For example, the step for a double-team block, or a trap block, or a cross-block. Backfield steps can also be coached with this kind of a drill. While we are interested in only the initial step, we must emphasize quickness, balance and proper position. It is an excellent practice to teach the linemen to exaggerate that initial step even though in actual use it may only be a short jab step. By exaggerating it's length, the execution becomes easier in a game situation. Therefore, putting all the basic fundamentals together, we have: a perfect stance, taking the initial step in the proper way and right direction, good initial contact with the proper surface of the body, acceleration of the feet on contact and, finally, rising-up on contact to take the defender past the point of attack.

THE FAR SHOULDER BLOCK

The techniques used in executing this type of shoulder block are basically the same as those described for the near shoulder block and are fundamentally the same techniques used in all forms of blocking. The front part of the chest, the forearms and the shoulder are the main contact surfaces used in the far shoulder block. An important note for the coach is that even though the far shoulder is being used as a blocking surface, the near foot is still the vital first step in getting to the defender. The major difference lies in the particular situation that calls for the use of this technique as opposed to other techniques. The far shoulder is defined as that shoulder farthest away from the defender to be blocked. A defender who is aligned to the blocker's right side would be attacked with the blocker's *left* shoulder; and conversely, if the defender were on the left side, he would be attacked with the blocker's *right* shoulder in a far shoulder block.

The far shoulder block derives its advantages from the fact that by its very nature it forces the blocker's body across and in front of the defender's route. This action, executed with some degree of force, prevents the defender from penetrating across the line of scrimmage and destroying the backfield action. For this reason it is not the kind of block that can be used to move defenders over a great distance, but rather to nullify their hard charge. Some practical applications of the far shoulder block are:

1. Blocking gap defenses.
2. Blocking for extra points and field goals.
3. Filling in for a pulling lineman.
4. Blocking down on the goal line, or in short yardage situations.
5. All plays such as sweeps, counters and reverses that take longer to develop than dives or quick openers.

In Diagrams 1-10 and 1-11, the blockers are using the "far" shoulder block to cutoff defensive penetration.

The Far Shoulder Block

1. Starting position showing the defenders in the gaps.

Diagram 1-10

2. Note how their initial steps are in the direction of the defenders. The routes through the gaps are sealed off and penetration stopped. The shaded area indicates that each blocker is using a far shoulder block with the right shoulder.

Diagram 1-11

THE RUN-THROUGH BLOCK

So far we have discussed one-on-one blocking types as they pertain to situations on the line of scrimmage, however, there are times when a blocker will be faced with a one-on-one situation in the open field. The people most likely to face this situation are the wide receivers and the ends whose job it is to block defensive halfbacks on most plays. Another time when this situation arises is when an interior lineman pulls out of the line to trap a defender or lead the ball-carrier around the end on a wide play. For all these lineman in this type of a situation, teach a technique of blocking called the run-through block.

When this situation presents itself to the blocker, he is faced with several conditions that are far different from blocking at the line of scrimmage. For one thing, the defender is standing on his feet and already in motion. Secondly, the defender has a great deal of area with which he can elude the blocker and still recover in time to make the tackle. Thirdly, both the blocker and the defender have built up sufficient momentum to make the impact of collision greater than it would normally be if contact were made at the line of scrimmage. Putting all these factors into consideration, the coach should recognize the importance for teaching this phase of line play with the utmost care and precision.

The term run-through is used to describe the nature of the block desired. Because of the presence of velocity and momentum between blocker and defender, it is not enough to merely hit or make contact with the defender. The coach must impress on his blocker the necessity for actually "running through" the man he must block, otherwise he will suffer more from the shock of initial contact. The ideal situation is to teach your blockers to run-through their opponents and then continue looking upfield for someone else to block. A blocker who executes this technique properly will be able to block more than one defender on a given play. The following coaching points should be stressed to make the run-through block effective:

1. The blocker must be square with the defender before he makes contact. A hit from the side lacks power, and the defender may be able to slide by or elude the block.

2. The blocker should use his eyes as an aiming device and direct it at the defender's chest. This will help prevent blocking too low which in turn causes the blocker to fall to his knees.

3. Once contact is made, the blocker accelerates and rises-up on his block, thus running-through the defender.

Obviously, the run-through block is nothing more than the drive block technique used in the open field. It is the only true way to block the defensive halfbacks and safetymen on wide plays. Coaches can drill this technique with air-shields and with live defenders by creating real situations under controlled conditions. Diagrams 1-12 through 1-14 depict how these may be implemented in the practice session.

Drilling for the Run-Through Block with a Simulated End-Run

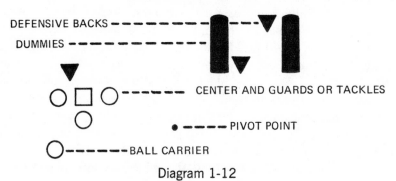

Diagram 1-12

1. The starting position for the run-through drill.

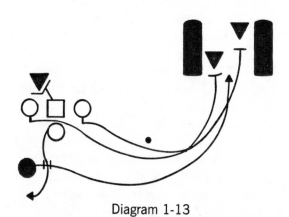

Diagram 1-13

2. The correct initial steps are encouraged throughout the drill. Also, the blockers must approach the line of scrimmage with shoulders square facing opponent.

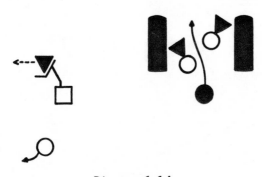

Diagram 1-14

3. Contact must be made squarely with a drive
   block. Blockers then accelerate and rise-up to
   complete the technique and open the running
   lane.

The blocking techniques in this chapter form the basis for all forms of blocking in a one-on-one situation and stress the necessity for sound fundamentals. In the next chapter we will present blocking types that combine the efforts of two or more blockers at the point of attack. We call these techniques, "combination blocking."

chapter 2

Combination Blocking

Combination blocking is a term that we use for describing the effective blocking of more than one lineman executed at the point of attack. It is understood that while each man involved in the block is performing some variation of the one-on-one techniques described in Chapter 1, nevertheless, the success of the play is dependent upon the combined actions of all blockers involved. Combination blockers are used to add optional ways of blocking various defenses for the same play. In this way a team may gear itself for a set number of plays and run them with the utmost execution against all defenses by simply changing or redefining the blocking combinations to be used. As part of a regular set of running plays, combination blocks make possible such plays as the simple dive, the option, the veer, the sweep, the trap, the draw, the isolation and many other plays that add to a well-rounded offensive arsenal. In addition, there are times when combination blocks are necessary to overcome deficiencies, or to overcome some sort of disadvantage. An elaborate list of how combination blocks might serve your offensive system follows:

1. To add power at the point of attack as in a short yardage situation or on the goal line.
2. To get more blockers to the point of attack than there are defenders (as in the sweep or option).
3. To aid in adjusting the blocking to variations in defensive sets (as in the case of multiple defensive teams).

4. To help one blocker who may be weaker than his defensive opponent in a one-on-one situation.

5. To help overcome the power and skill of one or more particular defenders.

Regardless of how the combinations of blocks are used, the basic fundamentals are still the same as those for one-on-one techniques. Every blocker must begin with the perfect three-point stance; every blocker must take the correct initial step; every blocker must fire-out quickly; every blocker must make good initial contact; and every blocker must rise-up and accelerate on contact. In this chapter we will describe some common types of combination blocks and also diagram them against various defensive sets.

THE DOUBLE-TEAM BLOCK

Double-team blocking is essential if power is to be a part of your offense. The double-team block assigns two blockers to move one defender. It's purpose is to create an opening at the point of attack that is too wide for a pursuing defender to fill alone. It also has the effect, if executed properly, of sealing off pursuit from the inside by linebackers. Certain offensive formations lend themselves to the use of double-team blocking more than others; however, the following diagrams illustrate the most common uses of the double-team block with the formations and backfield actions that go with the specific play-types. (See Diagrams 2-1 through 2-4.)

One special characteristic of the double-team block is brought out by Diagrams 2-1 through 2-4, that being that any pair of linemen can execute this technique on any given play. The factor that decides which pair of blockers will use the block is the defensive setup. In several instances in the diagrams, the linebackers are left unblocked by direct assignment. The intention with these types of plays is to provide the ball carrier with maximum daylight at the immediate point of attack for such cases as short yardage or goal line efforts. In situations such as these, a linebacker's tackle three yards off the line of scrimmage is usually meaningless anyway. Furthermore, the proper execution of the double-team should make pursuit from the inside very difficult.

TERMS CAN BE CONFUSING

Although it is comfortable for us to speak in terms of double-team

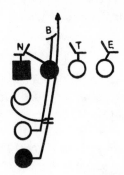

Diagram 2-1: I Formation.
Isolation play with guard/center double-team.

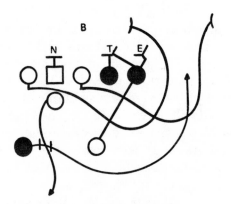

Diagram 2-2: Split-T Formation.
Sweep play with tackle/end double-team.

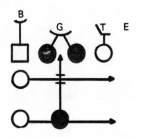

Diagram 2-3: T Formation.
Dive/Option series with guard/tackle double-team.

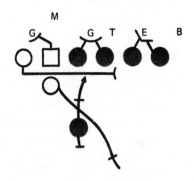

Diagram 2-4: Unbalanced Formation.
Draw-trap play with two powerful double-team
blocks.

blocking, many coaches are more familiar with such terms as "two-on-one," "the shoot block," "the power block," "post-and-lead" and "post-and-drive" blocking. Our feeling about these different terms is that they have more meaning for the coach than they do for the players. As the diagrams will show, each of these techniques fits our definition of double-team blocking. The major difference in their names is due to the fact that they are used against different defensive positions. The confusion among players will arise when an opponent uses multiple defenses, and the blockers see several different sets for one particular play. This forces them to think, "Am I the post man or the drive man on this block?" "Do I use a power block or a shoot block against this defensive set?" The questions and the doubt go on to cause hesitation which destroys the block from the very first. Diagrams 2-5 thru 2-8 will illustrate my point.

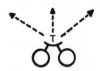

Diagram 2-5: Two-On-One Block.

This technique is executed on a defender aligned in the gap between blockers. The purpose of the block is simply to move the defender out of the point of attack in any direction possible.

Diagrams 2-6 through 2-8 show how an effective double-team block will seal-off the linebackers pursuit and force him to loop around the blockers.

By sticking to the basic terminology that states exactly what we want on every play, against every defense, the blockers are not concerned so much with direction, or specific technique. Regardless of the position of the defender, if a double-team block is called for, the two blockers involved will execute their assignments. To illustrate the difference between usage of terminology that changes with the defense, and the consistency of using one term, the diagrams show blocking for one special play against two different defenses. In Dia-

Diagram 2-6: The Shoot Block.

This technique is executed against the defender aligned on the inside shoulder of the inside blocker. The purpose of the block is to force the defender deep to the inside creating a large gap at the point of attack and sealing off inside pursuit from the linebacker.

Diagram 2-7: The Power Block.

This block-type is executed against the defender who is aligned head on the inside blocker. The inside blocker must setup the defender so that the outside blocker can come down on him and in unison, turn the defender down the line of scrimmage to open the hole and seal off inside pursuit from the linebacker.

Diagram 2-8: The Post and Lead Block.

This technique is executed against the defender who is aligned outside of the point of attack and must be taken inside. The outside blocker does the "setting up" in the *post* portion of the block, while the inside blocker must *lead* around to drive the defender to the inside.

grams 2-9 and 2-10, the blockers have to use entirely different techniques, while in Diagrams 2-11 and 2-12, the blockers execute the same double-team block on the same defender. The result shows that the defender goes a different way when blocked with the double-team.

With this simplification in terminology the blockers are concerned only with the technique of their block. The four considerations are as follows:

1. How is the initial step to be taken towards the defender?
2. What part of my body will I use for initial contact?
3. What must I do to prevent the defender from penetrating?
4. Which is the easiest possible direction for me to move the defender?

Fullback Off Tackle Play

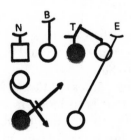

Diagram 2-9

Power block vs. 5-2 defense.

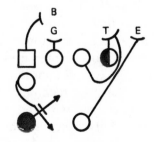

Diagram 2-10

Post and lead block vs. 4-4.

Fullback Off Tackle Play

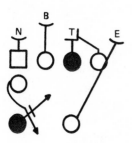

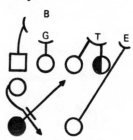

Diagram 2-11   Diagram 2-12

Use of simple double-team blocking makes assignments less confusing and produces the same
desired results, i.e., maximum daylight at the
point of attack.

FIVE STEPS TO DOUBLE-TEAM BLOCKING

The techniques of double-team blocking can be described as an
expanded form of two separate one-on-one blocks "combined" on the
same defender. Both linemen must step directly towards the defender on their first step with the near foot. This step is the first vital
technique so essential if the double-team block is to be soundly executed. It has the effect of getting the blockers to the defender quickly
and also of closing the gap between them so that the defender will not
be able to split them apart.

The second technique is learning which part of the body should
be used in making initial contact. Both blockers should make contact
with a drive block (see Chapter 1). We encourage this for the simple
reason that circumstances may arise where one of the blockers does
not get to his assignment. If this happens, for whatever reason, each
blocker must be prepared to take the defender one-on-one, and this is
our best way of handling the one-on-one situation.

The third technique can not be introduced unless both blockers
are in contact with the defender. Assuming that both blockers have
successfully executed the first two techniques, they must combine
their efforts to complete the block. Since the two blockers have made
contact, the seam or gap between them must be closed to prevent the
defender from splitting them. The desired effect is to have two blockers moving as one unit. In order to accomplish this the blockers are

taught to "feel" each other's presence and slide off their drive blocks and resort to a near shoulder block. The idea of feeling each other's presence is not an abstract thing, because the points of contact between the two blockers are the inside shoulders and hips. When these areas are properly connected, the gap between the blockers is closed. Daily drilling at very slow speeds to develop this feel for each other's presence is the only way the technique can be mastered. The coach should start the blockers off with a walk-through technique for many trials. Gradually the tempo increases until the desired results are obtained in live scrimmage work.

The fourth technique teaches the blockers how to move the defender the easiest way possible. In actuality, as the blockers make contact with the defender they have a fairly good idea which way they will try to take him. The defender who plays head-on one of the blockers will probably slant one way or another, and this defender will simply be taken the way he wants to go, beyond the point of attack. Defenders who remain stationary will be driven in the direction of least resistance, while the defender who plays in the gap between the blockers will be driven straight back.

The fifth and final technique is the most important. Many years ago the double-team was successful if it simply buried the defender right where he was, but with today's sophisticated defensive techniques, such as spinning out, slanting, and reading, offensive blockers must follow through after contact and maintain their blocks until the play is whistled dead by the referee. In order to complete the follow-through in the double-team block, we drill our blockers daily on the technique of rising-up and accelerating. This drill does not add a new dimension to our daily routine because it is a desirable aspect of every type of block in our system. In summary then, the techniques of expert double-team blocking are:

1. Both blockers must take the correct initial step.
2. Both blockers attack the defender with a drive block anticipating that they will have to block him alone.
3. Both blockers "feel" for each other's shoulder and hip to close the gap between them.
4. Both blockers work as a single unit to move the defender in the easiest direction.
5. Both blockers must rise-up and accelerate as a means of following through.

THE CROSS BLOCK

In this day of modern football, defenses have learned how to combat many one-on-one blocking patterns by showing the offense a variety of alignments. The relative success with which you are able to run your plays against these ever changing alignments depends largely on how you are able to adjust your blocking patterns. One of the simplest ways to achieve this adjustment is to switch the blocking assignments between two linemen at the point of attack. In effect, the defense has probably shifted in such a way as to deprive blockers of an easy angle of approach for their block; therefore, switching the assignments between blockers should give the advantage back to the offensive linemen. The act of switching assignments between two blockers is called cross blocking and a clear example of it's use and effectiveness can be seen in Diagrams 2-13 through 2-15.

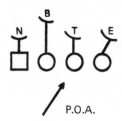

Diagram 2-13

Sound one-on-one blocking vs. 5-2 regular.

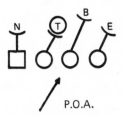

Diagram 2-14

"Eagle" adjustment makes one-on-one blocking inadequate on defensive tackle.

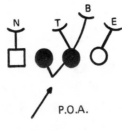

P.O.A.

Diagram 2-15

Cross block adjusts nicely for this play vs. "eagle"
shift.

Note how the play being run in all situations is the same, yet the
blocking patterns must change in order to adjust to the defensive
shifts. If the blocking pattern does not change, as against the "eagle"
alignment, then the defensive tackle will not be blocked adequately.
A simple switching of assignments as in the cross block makes the
necessary adjustment.

WHO MOVES FIRST?

Since cross blocking involves two linemen, the problem of which
man moves first arises. In order to distinguish the two different possibilities, we use two separate terms, the first of which is the "fold"
technique. "Fold" describes that type of cross block where the outside lineman will step first towards the defender and the inside lineman will step around behind him. The relationship of outside and
inside between linemen is explained as follows:

1. If the center and guard are to execute the fold technique, the
   guard is the outside lineman and moves first.
2. Between guard and tackle, the tackle is considered outside
   and he moves first.
3. Where the end and tackle are involved in the fold technique,
   the end will move first as he is outside the tackle.

Diagrams 2-16 through 2-18 clearly show the routes taken by the
outside and the inside linemen in the three combinations just discussed for the fold technique.

The advantages of using the fold technique in these three exam-

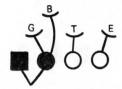

Diagram 2-16: Center/Guard Fold.

Diagram 2-17: Guard/Tackle Fold.

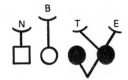

Diagram 2-18: Tackle/End Fold.

ples should be obvious. First, in the center/guard point of attack, the center is able to execute a one-on-one block against a defender playing head-on, but because he must snap the ball before moving too far forward, he will have difficulty blocking a quick linebacker. Therefore, since the fold technique requires that he move second in the crossing action, it is more conducive to his blocking assignment. The main objective in crossing the blockers is to relieve them of the difficulty of a straight one-on-one situation where they might get beat by a bigger, stronger defender. The cross block gives each blocker the extra advantage of the angle approach as well as the "sneak attack".

Cross blocking has another side which will be discussed subsequently, but it's important to note that just as in the case of the one-on-one techniques and as in the case of the double-team block, all basic drills and training methods can be used to drill for the cross block. The coach should begin his earliest training as a walk-through drill and gradually work up to full-speed contact work. A second method of cross blocking is called "bingo" in our system.

Bingo

This technique, which we have come to call bingo, is no more than the fold technique in reverse. In this crossing technique, the inside lineman will move first and the outside lineman will step around behind him. Diagrams 2-19 through 2-21 show how the combinations work against different defenses.

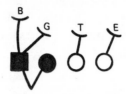

Diagram 2-19: Center/Guard Bingo.

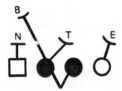

Diagram 2-20: Guard/Tackle Bingo.

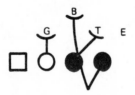

Diagram 2-21: Tackle/End Bingo.

To remind the reader, the following list of coaching points will aid in the teaching of these two techniques.

1. Regardless of whether the technique is fold or bingo, the first man to move must step in the proper direction with his near foot.
2. Each blocker should attack the defenders with a sound drive block.
3. The second blocker takes a jab step with his near foot to allow

the first man to pass avoiding collision. There is no waiting or delay per se, this jab step is sufficient.

4. Upon contact, both blockers must rise-up and accelerate.

Once the timing of the steps is perfected, these variations of cross blocking can be used against all defenses in any offensive series. The best example of this statement is to mention the fullback veer play off the wishbone formation and triple option series. As most coaches know, many blocking assignments in the triple option consist of basic blocking with no pulling and little combination blocking. Defenses have risen to the occasion and reset their tackles, lineback-

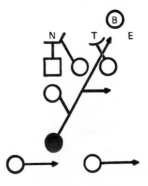

Diagram 2-22

Basic blocking pattern for triple option series leaves linebacker unblocked in vital position.

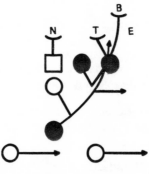

Diagram 2-23

Guard/tackle fold technique nullifies advantages of Eagle alignment.

ers and ends into an eagle alignment to stop the fullback veer. In Diagrams 2-22 and 2-23, we see how basic blocking against the eagle alignment breaks down and how the use of a crossing technique, fold, nullifies the defense and improves the same play.

WHAT DETERMINES THE USAGE OF FOLD
AS OPPOSED TO BINGO?

There are several key factors that make this decision relatively easy once they are understood.

1. The point of attack determines which pair of linemen are going to be involved in cross blocking. The linemen must know without a doubt which areas or holes are their responsibility. (See Diagram 2-24.)

Diagram 2-24

2 hole = center/guard; 4 hole = guard/tackle; and 6 hole = tackle/end.

2. The blocker who will move first is the blocker who is not covered head-on by a defensive lineman. The blocker who is covered head-on is the disadvantaged blocker, and he will jab step around behind his teammate. Fold or bingo are just terms that determine where the head-on defender is lined up. (See Diagrams 2-25 and 2-26.)

     The point of attack for both
situations is the same.

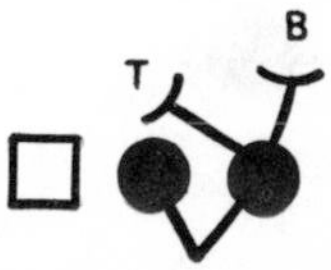

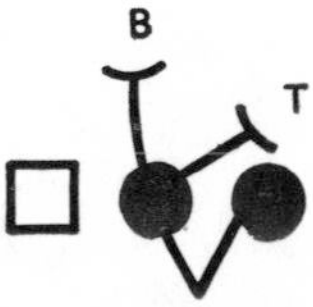

Diagram 2-25: Fold Block.   Diagram 2-26: Bingo Block.

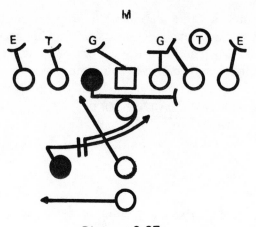

Diagram 2-27

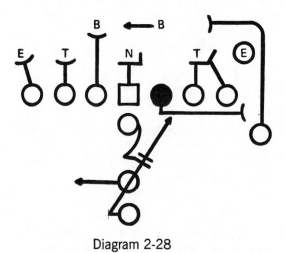

Diagram 2-28

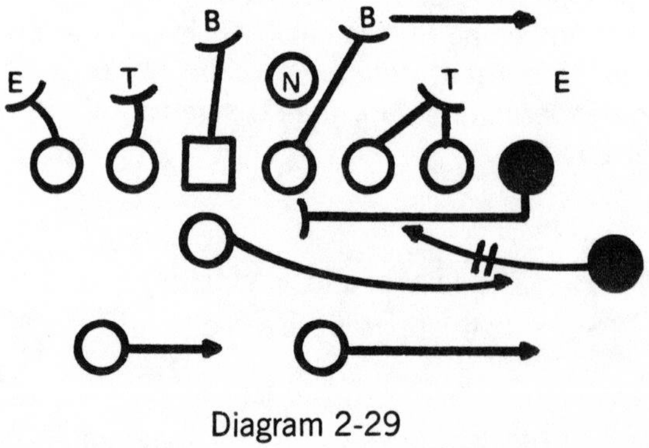

Diagram 2-29

THE TRAP BLOCK

The trap block is named after the type of play rather than as a special blocking technique. The play is used to "sucker" a hard charging lineman to penetrate the line of scrimmage without blocking him with the blocker who is head-on him. The actual block comes from an offensive lineman who pulls from the opposite side of the line and makes contact from the blind side. By the time the defender realizes what is going to happen it is usually too late to do anything more than take on the blocker one-on-one. Therefore, once again, we are describing a special one-on-one technique of blocking.

TRAP SEQUENCES

Some typical trap plays have been diagrammed below showing how defenders in all positions may be "trapped," and how any one of several different offensive linemen can execute the trap technique. (See Diagrams 2-27 through 2-29.)

The trap as a play is only as good as the trap technique of blocking. There are many coaching points that must be understood before the trap can be run with its full effectiveness. The first coaching point is the manner in which the all important first step is taken. As in every other block we have talked about thus far, and like each block we will discuss in future chapters, the blocker must take his initial step in the immediate direction of the defender's position with his near foot. In the case of a trap block, if the blocker is going to trap right, he must step initially to the right with his right foot. The procedure for trapping to the left is completely reversed. In addition to stepping in the right direction and with the proper foot, the trapper must step *into* the line of scrimmage, taking an inside route to the defender. The importance of this step can not be overlooked, for if the blocker fails to take an inside position on his first step, he will be completely out of position to trap the defensive player who waits or reads at the line of scrimmage. The trap block should be coached against three defensive charge routes, as follows:

1. The worst route the defender can take is *no* route at all. This is the "waiter."

2. The second most dangerous route is the one-step read which puts the defender right on the line of scrimmage.

3. The third route is the best route for trap blocking. This is the over-penetration that goes deeper than the backfield.

The trapper must assume that the defender will take the worst possible route and compensate for this by stepping into the line of scrimmage to give himself the best angle shot at the defender. Diagrams 2-30 through 2-35 show how the blocker's route will hurt or help him in trapping the defender in the three possible situations.

Diagrams 2-30 through 2-32 illustrate that the lateral pulling route taken by the trapper is only effective against two of the three possible defensive charges. In Diagrams 2-33 through 2-35, note how the trapper takes an inside angle into the line and is always on target to block the defender regardless of the charge he makes.

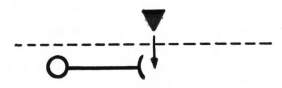

Diagram 2-30

Defender reads but can still be trapped by blocker.

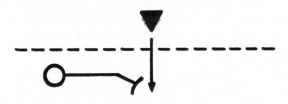

Diagram 2-31

Defender over-penetrates and is easily trapped.

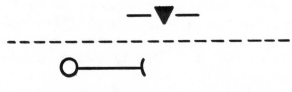

Diagram 2-32

Defender waits or slants and can not be trapped with this angle.

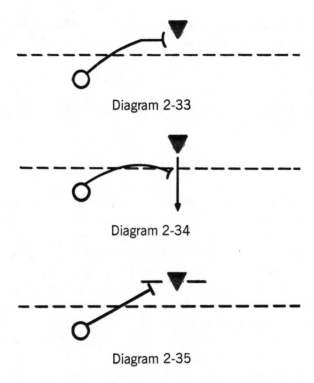

Diagram 2-33

Diagram 2-34

Diagram 2-35

The inside angle taken by the trapping lineman accommodates all types of defensive charges and slants.

INITIAL CONTACT IS IMPORTANT

Contact is the next most important phase of the trap block and there are several ways that contact can be made with success. The first and foremost technique is of course, the drive block. Since the blocker and defender are relatively far away from each other, there is the distinct possibility that the defender could react and avoid the trap block by backing up or moving out of the way. By using the drive block, the trapping lineman is assuring himself maximum visibility and maximum contact area. Should the defender try to slip away from contact, the blocker can always slide off into a shoulder block and accelerate with still a good surface area for driving.

The second way that the trap block may be executed is with the near shoulder block. The problem with shoulder blocking on the trap is that the blocker may use the wrong shoulder. When trapping to the right, if the blocker were to use his left shoulder, the defender would easily slip to the inside and destroy the play. Therefore, when coaching the use of a shoulder block for trapping, this simple rule must be memorized: "In order to TRAP to the right, step first with the right foot and block with the right shoulder"; "TRAP left . . . step left . . . left shoulder."

A FINAL WORD ABOUT PRECISION

At this point we should emphasize the need for precision in the execution of combination blocks. Whether the block involves a double-team, a cross, a short trap or a long sweep, since the techniques have become more complicated, the time spent perfecting these techniques should increase proportionally. The reasoning is basic: If more than one blocker is executing more than one technique, all of which are vital to the success of one particular play, the chances for error have increased greatly and the success of the play is in jeopardy without precision developed through adequate practice time. Therefore, we do not recommend that your entire offensive system and play-types be decided by combination blocking, but that whichever plays do require these combined techniques receive sufficient practice and drill time.

chapter 3

Individual Blocking Techniques

The old proverb, "Football is a game of blocking and tackling," is very true, but neither blocking nor tackling alone make up good football. A lineman who can block well because he is bigger and stronger than his opponent will eventually lose his advantage to a defender who is quicker and plays his position with finesse and technique. In modern football, defensive stars are not flat-footed in their stance, waiting to challenge a blocker in a man-on-man battle. Stunts, slants and loops are the order of the day, and if the offensive linemen are to keep pace with the defender's tactics, they too must develop blocking techniques and finesse. Realizing that football has become a game of techniques, we have adopted several blocking techniques that make blocking successful against the modern defensive weapons. We advocate the use of these techniques as a means for sophisticating the individual line play of your centers, guards, tackles and tight ends. Furthermore, it is hoped that once mastered, these techniques will be employed by your linemen at their own discretion. In this way, the defender is not only in doubt as to the point of attack, or the starting count, or who will block him, but also *how he will be blocked*. The only essential ingredient to full acceptance of these techniques is open-mindedness and common sense.

THE CARTWHEEL BLOCK

Defenders who play head-on a blocker are the most difficult people to block. This is true for several reasons:

1. If the defender is bigger and stronger than the blocker, we have a one-on-one mismatch.
2. Defenders who are head-on usually are in this position to execute some sort of stunt or slant.
3. The inexperienced offensive lineman tends to wait or hesitate, allowing the defender to beat him on the initial charge.
4. Since the defender is allowed to use his hands, the blocker's head and shoulders are prime targets for a quick shot at the snap of the ball.

The blocker most troubled by this situation is the offensive center, for unlike the other blockers, he must snap the football at the same time he fires-out to make contact. Another disadvantage that the center endures, is that most of the time the defender playing head-on him is very close to his nose. Unlike the guard's man or the tackle's man who are slightly off the ball, the center must be prepared to take a defensive shot immediately, and because of these factors many centers get beat by a good nose-guard's quick charge. Although the technique of cartwheel blocking can be used by any blocker who is faced with a head-on defender, we offer it as an individual technique for centers against the 5 man defense and the nose-guard.

The purpose of the cartwheel block is to nullify the defender's charge, avoid contact with the defender's hands and arms, and prevent the defender from pursuing the play. By no means, however, will this block move a defender very far or "blow" him out of the hole. If executed properly, the cartwheel block will eliminate the defender from the play entirely.

Execution of the cartwheel block is similar to the scramble block as far as contact and initial movement are concerned. The blocker must get his shoulders and helmet under the defender's groin area in a lunge or explosion off the line of scrimmage. At the instant contact is made the actual cartwheel action comes into use. The blocker whips his hips to the right or left, depending on which way the play is going, and makes a complete 180 degree turn on all fours. If the play goes to the right, then he whips his hips to the right, and conversely for a play that goes to the left. The term "cartwheel" emphasizes the necessity

N

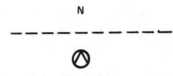

Diagram 3-1   The center vs. nose-guard.

Diagram 3-2   Initial contact made with scramble technique.

Diagram 3-3   The blocker now begins to whip or cartwheel his hips.

Diagram 3-4   The completed block shows the head and feet are 180 degrees from the original starting point and the defender is cut off from pursuit.

for the whipping action of the hips in order to bring the blocker around 180 degrees. This position prevents the defender from pursuing laterally to the point of attack. Diagrams 3-1 through 3-4 depict the steps in execution of the cartwheel technique.

Some coaching points should be stressed here if the cartwheel block is to be perfected:

1. Make initial contact with a scramble block.

2. Accelerate before turning the hips to cartwheel.

3. Whip the hips to the side of the point of attack until you are 180 degrees from where you started.

In the event that you notice the defender getting away from this block, there are two points that should be checked. First, it is possible that the blocker is too conscious of turning his hips and is not making proper initial contact first. He must scramble block his opponent first, *then*, cartwheel. The second thing to watch is whether or not the blocker is truly whipping his hips around the defender. The cartwheel technique should be so quick that the blocker actually leaves his feet in the process of whipping. He should not mistake this action for a crab-type walk.

The main idea of blocks and techniques like this is to teach your offensive lineman that brain can defeat brawn. No physical requirements are necessary for the cartwheel block, yet it is a valuable weapon to be used against the defender who lines up head-on and tries to out-muscle the blocker.

THE CHECK BLOCK

The check block is little more than a far shoulder block used on a *specific play* by a *specific lineman* with a *specific purpose*. The play type that requires the use of the check block is any play where one or more interior linemen pull out of the line to trap a defender or help lead plays that go around the end.

The specific lineman involved in check blocking is any lineman playing directly next to the pulling blocker on the side nearest the point of attack. Diagrams 3-5 through 3-7 show several play types

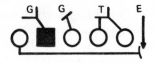

Diagram 3-5

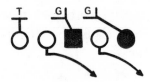

Diagram 3-6

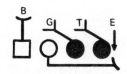

Diagram 3-7

where one or more linemen are required to pull out, and the shaded figure indicates that lineman who would be using the check block.

As the diagrams indicate, the check blocker is using this technique to prevent two things; first, to stop the penetration of the defender into the offensive backfield; and second, to stop the defender from pursuing the play laterally. These two purposes are not only specific, but also vital if the pulling lineman's block is to be effective.

Since the check block is nothing more than a far shoulder block, one might ask why the separate term? The reason is justified by the nature of the plays that require check blocking. For example, if we want our centers to block any defender playing head up on a pulling guard, we want him to stop the defender's penetration and pursuit. Having coached several different ways to block a man one-on-one, the center may try to use a drive block or a scramble block or even a near shoulder block to carry out his assignment. However, these types of blocks are not sufficient to achieve our two purposes. Therefore, instead of asking the blocker to remember that he must use the far shoulder technique, we encourage him to think of his assignment as a check block. By giving this term to the act of blocking for a pulling lineman, everyone is aware that only the far shoulder block will suffice. In the course of instructing the line in their blocking rules, we just include the term check block to mean the type of block used exclusively to block for a pulling lineman.

To reiterate the differences between the far shoulder block and the check block, we would say that the use of the far shoulder block is an option open to any blocker who feels that he can accomplish his assignment with it. But the check block is a precise block, mandatory in plays where one lineman must block the defender head-on a pulling lineman. The diagrams show how the check block serves all offensive lineman in different situations. (See Diagrams 3-8 through 3-10.)

A final technique that could add to the benefits of the check block would be the use of a cartwheel after contact. This would insure that the defender did not backoff the line of scrimmage and avoid the check block. Since all the techniques of one-on-one blocking tend to overlap a great deal, the line coach should encourage the use of such techniques as an added part of each lineman's weapons system.

THE SWEEP BLOCK—PRO STYLE

The sweep, or end-run as it is more commonly known, is as old as football itself. The theory of the sweep is to attack the flank of the

Diagram 3-8

The left guard will pull out of the line while the center must check the defender's penetration and pursuit.

Diagram 3-9

Note how the first step of the center and the guard seem to mesh, allowing both blockers to get to their assignments as quickly as possible.

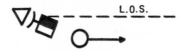

Diagram 3-10

The guard is completely out of the line now, and the center has stopped the defender's penetration. Note how the check blocker is using the far shoulder block. (Shaded area).

defense with more blockers than the defense can handle. Outnumbering the defenders is of prime importance to the success of the sweep, and this can be accomplished by pulling one or more of the interior linemen and having them lead the ball carrier around the end. The best executors of the sweep are the professional athletes and coaches who have the natural talent to intensify the devastating effect of this powerful play. Our contention is, however, that the techniques involved in running the sweep properly are wrapped-up almost entirely in the way the offensive linemen pull to lead the ball-carrier around the end. These techniques are taught in every pro football camp and can be adapted to the high school program if the coach's philosophy entertains the value of the sweep as an offensive weapon. We will further state, that no coach should waste the time of his staff or players by running any other facsimile of a sweep unless these special techniques are employed. The following diagrams illustrate several different offensive sets and how a sweep may be run from them (See Diagrams 3-11 and 3-12.)

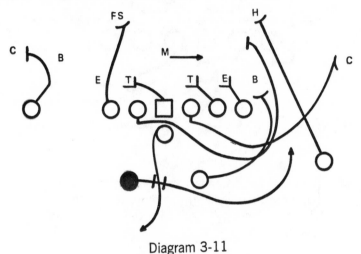

Diagram 3-11

Pro sweep vs. 6-1 Defense.

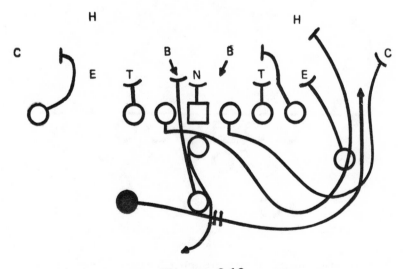

Diagram 3-12

Wing-T sweep vs. 5-2 defense.

Before we explain the blocking techniques, it is essential that an explanation of how the defense will react to a sweep or any end-run be given. A schematic explanation is given below:

The defensive lineman must pursue the play laterally, down the line of scrimmage. (Diagram 3-13.)

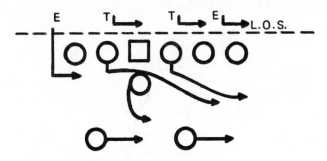

Diagram 3-13

The defensive secondary must rotate towards the
play from the outside-in, in order to prevent the
ball carrier from getting outside the last defender.
(Diagram 3-14.)

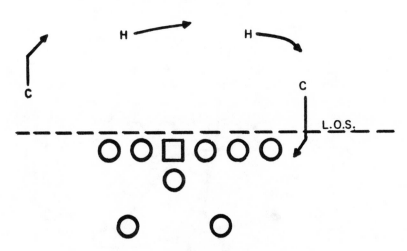

Diagram 3-14

The inside linebackers must pursue the play at
regular depth, laterally down the line of scrimmage. (Diagram 3-15.)

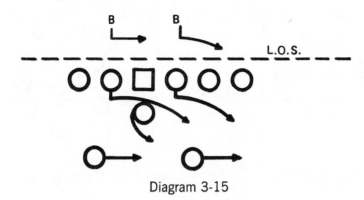

Diagram 3-15

The pursuit of the interior defensive linemen must be cut-off by the blocking of the onside offensive end and tackle and possibly the wingback in some formations. But the rotating secondary are the defenders who must be blocked by the pulling linemen. For our purposes, we will talk in terms of the guards as being the pulling linemen, although many teams run the sweep successfully by pulling a guard and a tackle. Regardless of which linemen get the assignment, the techniques and responsibilities are the same.

The most immediate problem is the defender who first appears on the outside of the end. This will be the defensive cornerback in a 4-spoke defense, and the outside end in a 3-spoke defense. This defender is supposed to come up and meet the play from the outside in. The lead blocker is responsible for taking this defender one-on-one and hopefully, kicking him *out*.

The second dangerous defender will be coming from the inside. He will be either the middle linebacker or the middle safety, depending on the assignment given to the wing or flanker-back. This defender is the responsibility of the trailing blocker and must be kept inside.

Diagrams 3-16 and 3-17 show the blocking scheme for the onside linemen and the lead blocker vs. two very common defenses. In Diagrams 3-18 and 3-19, the blocking schemes are designed against what is considered by most to be the pro defense and is most likely the best defense against the sweep. If you can block the pro defense effectively for the sweep, you should be able to block most any other defensive set.

The pulling lineman face several problems on sweep plays, all of which involve timing of some sort:

1. If they get to the point of attack too soon, their defender will

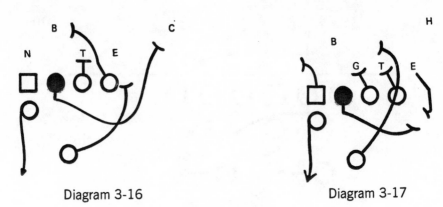

Diagram 3-16   Diagram 3-17

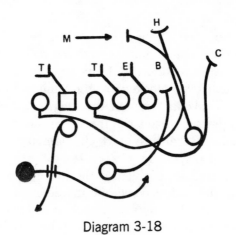

Diagram 3-18

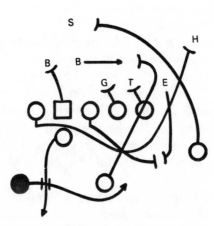

Diagram 3-19

have time to recover from the block and still get in on the tackle.

2. If they do not meet the defender squarely, and face-to-face, they may lose their balance and execute a sloppy block or lose the defender altogether.

3. If one of the pulling linemen gets to the point of attack before the other, the running back will be forced to commit himself to a direction too soon. Furthermore, the idea of outnumbering the defenders will have been defeated.

It is obvious from these coaching points that the proper execution of the sweep as a play in general, demands discipline and constant practice. The blockers' techniques are discussed below.

The lead blocker's first step must be with the near foot in the direction of the sweep, but back on an angle of forty-five degrees with the line of scrimmage. (See Diagram 3-20.)

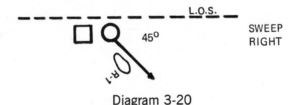

Diagram 3-20

His second step is what we call a "leveling-off" step that gets his entire body on this forty-five degree angle path with the line of scrimmage. (See Diagram 3-21.)

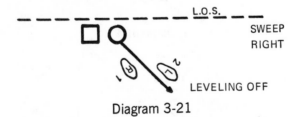

Diagram 3-21

The third step begins to round off his route to eventually bring his body square with the line of scrimmage heading upfield towards the goal line. (See Diagram 3-22.)

This series of steps represents an actual "loss" of about four yards. We refer to this as "getting depth," and it serves several purposes:

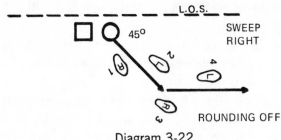

Diagram 3-22

1. It enables the back to catch up with the blocker so that they are together when the block is actually made.
2. It puts the blocker in a better position to see how the defense is rotating and to find his blocking assignment.
3. It enables the blocker to face his opponent squarely and make an effective run-through block.

This looping technique is a method that should also be taught to the ball carrier for the same reasons. Diagrams 3-23, 3-24, and 3-25

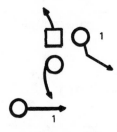

Diagram 3-23

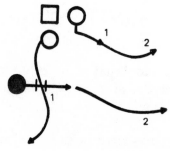

Diagram 3-24

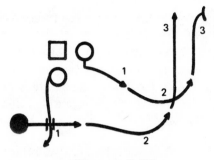

Diagram 3-25

show how all these steps put the lead blocker, defender and ball carrier in the right position at the right time.

The trailing blocker's techniques are exactly the same, save two points. The first point is that his initial two steps must be lateral so that he may clear the center's tail to allow the quarterback to make his pivot without colliding with him. This point differs from the initial steps taken by the lead blocker in that he will step off immediately on a forty-five degree angle. On the trailing blocker's third step, which will be with his near foot, he will begin the forty-five degree angle route taken by the lead blocker. From that point on he follows the same steps as the lead blocker until he gets to the line of scrimmage. The diagram helps clarify the actual steps taken by the trailing blocker. (See Diagram 3-26.)

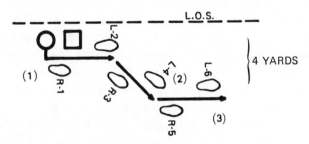

Diagram 3-26

1. The number (1) shows the first step taken with the right foot to get the blocker out of the line. The second step taken with the left foot gets the blocker past the center's tail and allows the QB to pivot without collision.

2. The number (2) shows the steps taken in order to get depth required for timing. These are the same steps as those taken by the lead blocker.

3. The number (3) represents the "leveling-off" steps taken by the blocker so that he may approach the line of scrimmage with body and shoulders square.

As he approaches the line of scrimmage, the trailing blocker should be almost side-by-side with the lead blocker and to his inside. (See Diagram 3-27.)

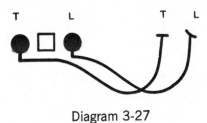

Diagram 3-27

The trailing blocker must be conscious of pursuit from the inside, so as soon as he is facing up-field towards the goal line he must use his eyes and find the first enemy jersey to come from the inside. A technique we have used successfully to make certain that the trail blocker looks inside is to have him put his inside hand down on the ground and turn or pivot on it to the inside. Since the entire sweep play demands precision and discipline, it is one time we do not simply block the "first enemy jersey seen." Each man has a precise assignment and must carry out his technique until it can no longer be executed. For example, we do not tell the blockers *whom* to block, but we insist that they are in a definite position *where* they are to block. Namely, the lead blocker looks to the *outside* once he clears the end. Furthermore, both blockers must use the sweep technique in order to get where we want them. Unless these techniques and disciplines are perfected the sweep will not be successful, and by "successful," we mean it must average at least four yards per carry.

THE HOOK BLOCK

The final type of individual technique is one that allows the tight end to block the defensive end on wide plays such as options and quick pitches. As a technique, however, we think that all linemen should learn the proper execution of the hook block in the event that they may decide to use it in a given situation.

The hook block is so named because it's objective is to prevent a defender who is already lined up on the blocker's outside to pursue to the outside. The blocker is attempting to take a defender who is aligned to his outside, to the inside. Normally, we do not ask our blockers to take a defender in any particular direction, but rather, take the defender in the direction he wants to go. But as you will see in the few play-types that are diagrammed, hook blocking techniques can aid in the execution of some very quick and devastating plays. (See Diagrams 3-28 and 3-29.)

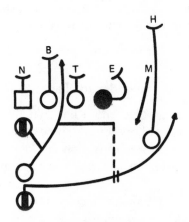

Diagram 3-28

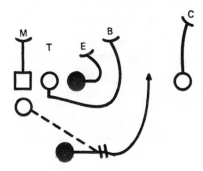

Diagram 3-29

The basic problem in situations where the hook block is desirable is position. The blocker is in a very bad position to be taking the defender *in*. Therefore, the blocker's initial step will again be vital. He must step perfectly laterally on a parallel with the line of scrimmage, towards the defender. Some blockers may even find it beneficial to step back on the same forty-five degree angle route that the pulling linemen used for the sweep block. The important thing is not to step directly at the defender, for in all probability he will be charging across the line of scrimmage, even if only one step, and this will destroy any chance the blocker had of hooking him. By taking this initial step, the blocker is giving himself better position on the defender and is also forcing the defender to make a choice as to where to charge. By stepping out or even back, the blocker has opened an alley to the inside that many defensive players will take. Therefore, we see that this position step has a two-fold purpose:

1. It puts the blocker in a better position to hook the defender to the inside.
2. It influences the defender to charge to the inside.

Once the advantage of position has switched to the blocker, he has a choice of two types of one-on-one block to use. Keeping in mind that his assignment requires only that he keep the defender from pursuing to the outside, he can use the far shoulder block or the cartwheel block.

If the far shoulder block is used the description of the entire blocking pattern for a blocker whose defensive counterpart was on his right would be as follows:

1. Step back or laterally with your right foot first, giving the defender an inside route to influence him to the inside.
2. Your next step should take you on a route towards the defender's outside hip. Your aiming device is your eyes.
3. Make contact with your *left* shoulder, forearm and side of helmet, accelerate and rise-up to turn the defender.

THE INFLUENCE BLOCK FOR TRAP PLAYS

We mentioned the word "influence" in the preceding section in the discussion of the hook block. The term is descriptive of the way offensive linemen can overcome the reading technique of defensive linemen. These reading tactics are also making it more and more difficult for teams to run trap plays or sweep plays with high degrees of success. The reading defender keys the blocker's moves and follows a set of rules that enable him to react to the proper pursuit angle without ever having to see the backfield action. Defenders who perform their reading skills well are extremely troublesome to offensive blocking that is anything other than straight one-on-one. The pulling lineman is an accurate key that will lead the defender to the play nine times out of ten since linemen are not often used for faking, as are backs.

Offensive blocking must sophisticate itself enough to compensate for the reading technique and once again take the advantage. By influencing the defender to do one thing, we can execute our blocking assignment more easily, and if the influence is good enough, the defender may in fact block himself. An example of how a reading defense can destroy the standard trap play is diagrammed below. (See Diagram 3-30.)

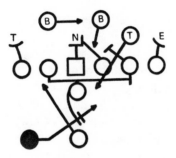

Diagram 3-30

The reading in the diagram can be explained as follows:

1. Both linebackers will key the guards in front of them. When a guard double-teams, the linebacker fills quickly; when a guard pulls, the linebacker pursues laterally and finds the ball.

2. The defensive tackle being trapped jams into the inside because he reads the offensive tackle in front of him going inside.

The result is that the onside tackle is forced to block a linebacker who is coming hard; the trapping guard must block a defender who is bearing down on him, shortening the distance between them; and finally, a linebacker is in pursuit and free to make the tackle at the point of attack.

Many coaches feel that the best way to counteract the difficulty is to do the trapping with a different lineman, namely, the offensive tackle, as shown in the diagram. But here again, the effects of reading are not being countered. (See Diagram 3-31.)

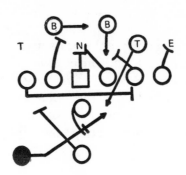

Diagram 3-31

In order to force the defense to use its reading techniques against itself, we teach the influence technique to the onside tackle. Since we are trapping the defender playing in front of him, we want our offensive tackle to force the defender to read incorrectly. We feel that this influence technique will benefit our play more than the double-team block most coaches use along with the trap itself, as in the case of the onside guard and center double-teaming the nose-guard. Our blockers sacrifice the double-team block and rely on well-executed one-on-one techniques to make the trap go.

Influencing can be done in several ways, the first way is a "brush-and-slide" type of influence. The blocker doing the influencing, usually the offensive tackle, will make a very slight contact with the defender we want to trap. In other words, he will "brush" him. The influence blocker then slides off the tackle *to the outside* and blocks the first defender to show. It is imperative that the influence blocker slide to the outside, for if the tackle is reading properly, he will slide out with our influence man. (See Diagrams 3-32 and 3-33.)

Another way we can influence the defender is by faking pass protection. The influence blocker will set up in pass protection style and may even yell, "pass, pass . . .," to make the defensive lineman

Brush-Style Influencing with Either Type of Trap

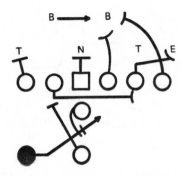

Diagram 3-32: Guard Trap vs. 5-2.

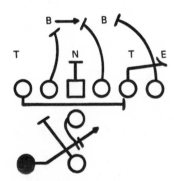

Diagram 3-33: Tackle Trap vs. 5-2.

think that a pass is in the making. Any good defensive lineman knows that on passes he must rush the quarterback, and this little bit of faking often causes the defender to actually straighten-up and over-charge through the line of scrimmage. This makes trapping ever so easy. This form of influence blocking, however, is also accompanied by a brush-and-slide technique, so that instead of going directly at the defender, the influence blocker now drops back and influences the defender to over-penetrate, and then he slides out and picks up his assignment. (See Diagram 3-34.)

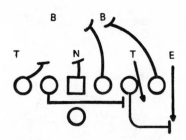

Diagram 3-34

The right tackle fakes pass protection blocking
and draws the defender in.

Finesse is the difference between those linemen who are good
blockers and those who are great ones. The individual lineman who
takes pride in his position should also have enough pride to practice
and develop these techniques. We contend that these techniques will
make the individual a more consistent blocker and a more confident
part of your offensive line.

part II

How to Block
Multiple Defenses

chapter 4

The Theories and Usage
of Multiple Defenses

Defensive football has found many ways to cope with variations in offensive sets and play series. Unlike the offense, the defense is in no way restricted by rules as to how many men may line up on the line of scrimmage, nor are they restricted as to how many backs are permitted to defend the secondary area. Therefore, it is more likely than not that any given team playing through a normal season will be faced with an entirely different defense each week. The defense has a greater supply of formations and alignments to throw at the offense than the offense has with which to attack the defense. It is even likely that through any one game, the offense may be faced with the challenge of blocking more than one defensive alignment. Teams that employ a variation of defensive fronts and adjustments do so to destroy the consistency of the offense's blocking schemes. When these multiple defensive teams present themselves on the field of play, the coach comes to realize just how effective his blockers are as thinkers and, more importantly, just how effective his team's rules are for blocking multiple defenses for his system of plays and passes. Teams that employ the concept of multiple defenses generally vary only the alignment of their run-prevention corps, that is, the defensive linemen and linebackers. The defensive backs are kept together throughout these variations up front and are of the type called "4-deep" or "3-deep" secondaries. The discussions in this chapter will deal with this premise and will use the 4-deep and 3-deep concepts as a basis for analyzing various defensive alignments. Upon completion of this part of the book, each coach should be able to give his blockers the necessary confidence that will enable them to block any defense, against any opponent for any offensive play.

DEFENSES WITH A 4-DEEP SECONDARY

The defenses to be discussed in this section use four defenders whose basic responsibility is to stop the passing game. The remaining

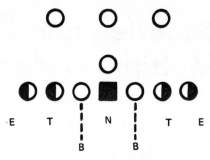

Diagram 4-1: Regular.

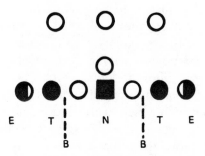

Diagram 4-2: Tight.

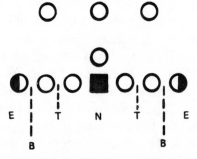

Diagram 4-3: Eagle.

seven defenders have the primary responsibility of run-prevention, and variations in the alignment of these seven men can cause the offensive lineman a great many headaches. Diagrams 4-1, 4-2, and 4-3 exhibit some of the more common variations of defenses with a 4-deep secondary.

THE 5-2 DEFENSE

The three diagrams are common variations of the 5-2 defense. In Diagram 4-1, the defensive tackles are aligned on the outside shoulder of their offensive counterparts. This position gives the defense strength off-tackle and helps the defender fight the double-team that he might encounter from the offensive tackle and tight end.

The tackles in this "regular" position are not generally given any other systematic charge routes other than to penetrate to a depth of two yards and then read and find the football. Consequently, we see very little, if any, slanting from the tackles in this variation of the 5-2. The defensive ends will play in either a two-point stance or a three-point stance and will be aligned on the outside shoulder of the tight end. Their responsibility is to force the running play to the inside if it is designed to go outside, and to force the play outside if it is designed to go inside. By stripping the ball carrier of his lead blockers, the defensive end may force an end-run to go inside, and at the same time, by jamming up the off-tackle hole, the defensive end may force an inside play to be over extended. Since he may be successful in either case, he has the responsibility of what we call "auxiliary contain." True and complete contain must come from the defensive corner backs with the responsibility called "aggressive contain." The twin linebackers are the only other members of the run-prevention corps that will vary their alignment. In the regular defense, the linebackers are three yards deep and head-on the offensive guards. In this position they are able to key the running backs and at the same time evade the blocking guards. By aligning head-on the guards, the linebackers are also able to read the pass situation more quickly since the guards will have to set up in pass protection immediately after the ball is snapped.

The "tight" variation, shown in Diagram 4-2, simply moves the defensive tackles in to a head-on position with the offensive tackles and moves the defensive ends to a semi-head-on position with the tight ends. In the tight alignment, a defense could play without special techniques and still cover all points of attack, or it could use slanting techniques very effectively. The head-on position of the defensive tackles and ends poses a great problem to the offensive blocker in normal situations, but the added attraction of slanting could prove to be too much for the ill-trained high school offensive lineman.

The final variation which is very common is the "eagle" look created by adjusting the linebackers and defensive tackles. Diagram 4-3 shows how the defensive tackles are moved into the offensive guard/tackle gaps and the linebacker is moved to an inside-shoulder aligment with the tight end. The defensive ends can maintain their regular or their tight alignment. The advantages of the eagle defensive set is that it lends itself very nicely to pass rushing by the tackles and pass defense by the linebackers. Since the defensive tackles are in the guard/tackle gap, they can penetrate and cause trouble more often than when they are playing head-on. The linebackers are in a good position to delay the tight end before he gets into his pass route and still cover the short hook zone on passes. Any combination of these various alignments can be used very effectively, especially if offensive tendencies can be predicted.

5-2 Stunts and Alignments

It is important for the offensive coach also to be an expert at defensive possibilities and strategy. We must not overlook the power and potential danger of the opponent who utilizes stunts a great deal. Diagrams 4-4 through 4-9 show the various stunts used by teams that favor the 5-2 defense and all its variations:

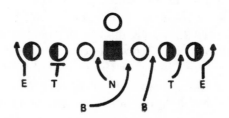

Diagram 4-4: 5-2 Regular, Double-Barrel Right (or Left).

Good passing blitz. The nose-guard, tackle and two linebackers attack the inside gaps.

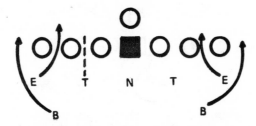

Diagram 4-5: 5-2 Eagle, Lightning.

Defensive ends and linebackers cross. Effective against option teams.

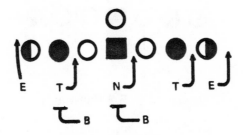

Diagram 4-6: 5-2 Regular, Slant Right, (or Left).

Slant technique is lateral step first, then into the next gap.

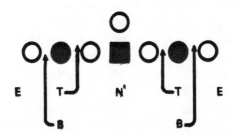

Diagram 4-7: 5-2 Tackle Stack.

Linebackers stack directly behind tackles, and, on the snap of the ball, the stacked pair slant in opposite directions into either gap.

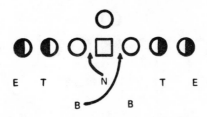

Diagram 4-8: 5-2 Regular, Cross Right, (or Left).

Involves only the nose-guard and one linebacker. Again the gaps are being attacked by this stunt.

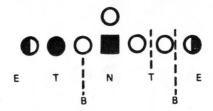

Diagram 4-9: 5-2 Half-and-Half.

One side is 5-2 regular, while the other side is "eagle". This alignment confuses blocking assignments for the offense.

THE 6-1 OR PRO DEFENSE

The 6-1 defense has been labeled as the pro defense for the simple reason that the vast majority of professional football teams employ it. It lends itself very well to both the run and the pass situation and is characterized by the one middle linebacker, two defensive tackles, two defensive ends, two outside linebackers, and the four-deep pass defense unit. Unlike the 5-2 defense, the pro defense gives both pass and run responsibility to its outside linebackers, who are the equivalent of defensive ends in the 5-2 alignment.

Basic Variations of the 6-1 Defense

Variations of the 6-1 alignment are not as vast as most other defensive sets. The most common ones are shown in Diagrams 4-10 through 4-14.

Diagram 4-10 depicts the regular alignment. The characteristics are that the middle linebacker (M) is head on the center and 3 yards

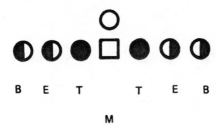

Diagram 4-10: 6-1 Regular.

Effective against the run, yet the only change from the 5-2 is that the nose-guard has moved to middle linebacker, and the twin linebackers have moved to a down position on the guards.

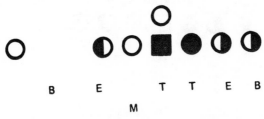

Diagram 4-11: 6-1 Over.

The defensive tackle is shifted "over" towards the tight end; the middle linebacker compensates by shifting left. Effective against teams that run to strong side.

Diagram 4-12: 6-1 Under.

The shift here is towards the split-end side, but is the same idea as the "over" shift. This alignment is effective against plays to the short side.

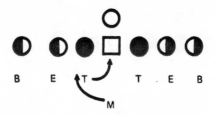

Diagram 4-13: 6-1 Cross Right or Left.

Crossing action between one tackle and the middle linebacker. An effective pass rush. This stunt can be run from the regular, over, or under alignments.

Diagram 4-14: 6-1 Loop.

Tackles slant out towards offensive tackle and defensive ends loop behind and come up the middle. For passing situations only!

off the ball; the defensive tackles are head-on the offensive guards; the defensive ends are in a down position and on the outside shoulder of the offensive tackle; the outside linebackers, who play the same role on running plays as the defensive ends in the 5-2 defense, are always in a two-point stance and slightly outside the tight end. If they are faced with a split end, the outside linebackers will drop off the line of scrimmage and play their run/pass responsibility from a depth of about 3 yards.

The regular defense again allows for maximum pursuit by the middle linebacker, since the defensive tackles and ends are playing so tight on their offensive opponents. In the regular alignment the middle linebacker should be able to reach any offensive opening from end to end. On running plays, this defense allows for seven run-responsible defenders, and yet on pass plays, there are four secondary defenders plus the two outside linebackers, making a total of six pass-responsible players.

Both the over and under variations represent ways that the middle linebacker can be shifted to the strength or weakness of the offensive set. In either case one of the defensive tackles moves over head-on the center while the linebacker moves to the position vacated by the defensive tackle. Diagrams 4-15 and 4-16 show how the over and under variations might help the defense against different offensive sets.

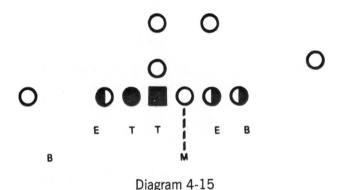

Diagram 4-15

"Under" here refers to the way in which the defensive tackle shifts. Since he shifts away from or under the tight end, the linebacker is able to shift to the strong side of the formation.

"Over" and "under" are calls usually assigned to the middle linebacker, and he can make these calls either in the defensive huddle or when the offense lines up over the ball. The directions refer to the position of the tight end. "Over" means shift towards the tight end, while "under" means shift away from him.

In either of the above situations the middle linebacker may have called the other shift. It simply depends on what he wants the new defensive alignment to accomplish.

THE 4-5 DEFENSE

Although the 4-5 alignment is relatively rare, it serves as a tremendous asset in situations when the offense must play catch-up football and passing is the only way it can accomplish this. Therefore, one finds the 4-5 setup used in prevention situations, and it should

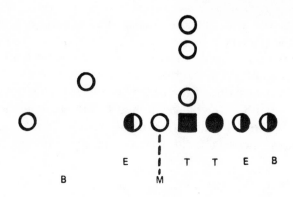

Diagram 4-16

"Over" is the call used against this offensive formation because the middle linebacker wants to
position himself in the best possible area to stop
the running game.

definitely be incorporated in some form in every team's defensive
arsenal. Diagram 4-17 shows how the 4-5 is set up against a typical
passing formation.

Without going into the details of the pass defense responsibilities, the run-prevention corps is relatively weak. However, the
defensive ends and tackles are in good position to challenge the pass
blockers ability to stop their rush, while all three linebackers can help
out on any pass-action running plays such as draws, screens or shovel
passes. It should also be noted that the depth of the five linebackers
may be varied depending on the yardage necessary for the offense to
successfully accomplish its goals. By distributing these people in different manners, the defense can practically cut off every passing zone
and make short running plays relatively ineffective.

DEFENSES WITH A 3-DEEP SECONDARY

Because the possibilities are greater and the combinations more
varied, defenses that employ the 3-deep pass defending team are
much more prevalent in today's football. These defenses have a total
of eight men to adjust to the run-prevention duties of defensive football. The first series of variations to be discussed are the 4-4 defenses.

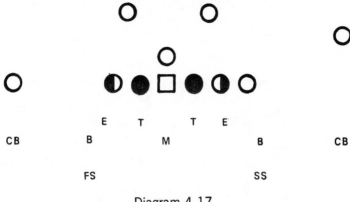

Diagram 4-17

4-5 prevent defense can be used effectively to stop the desperation pass or bomb.

THE 4-4 DEFENSES

Characteristic of the four man front are two defensive guards and two defensive tackles. These men are placed in a variety of positions as we shall demonstrate, but the novelty of these defensive sets is that the defensive ends are a major part of the pass defense team as well as the run-prevention unit. In order to select the proper personnel for the position of this type of defensive end, one must look for an individual who would normally make a good linebacker, a player who has the size and strength to play the run and the speed and skill to play the pass. Some variations of 4-4 defenses follow in Diagrams 4-18 through 4-23.

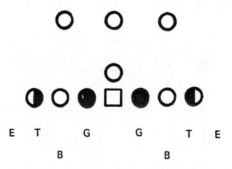

Diagram 4-18: The Wide Tackle Set.

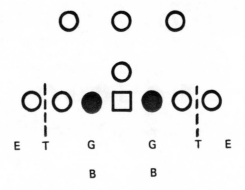

Diagram 4-19: 4-4 Stack.

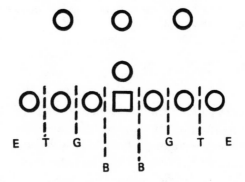

Diagram 4-20: Gap Set.

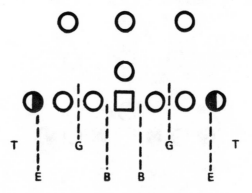

Diagram 4-21: Notre Dame 4-4.

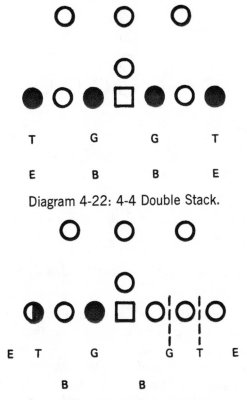

Diagram 4-22: 4-4 Double Stack.

Diagram 4-23: ½ and ½ Combo.

The major advantages of the various 4-4 alignments is that they lend themselves to a very good pass defense corps. As Diagram 4-24 indicates, the defense is able to cover all vital areas against passes without having to rotate. Some coaches find rotation a difficult technique to teach high school athletes, especially with the limited time and coaches available for this sort of instruction. For these reasons, 3-deep secondary defenses are an advantage. (Diagram 4-24.)

The disadvantages of defenses of this type are numerous if one looks at them objectively. First, any pass-responsible position is a "skill" position, much the same as quarterback is a "skill" position on offense. To expect to have at least seven players year after year with the ability to fit into these selective spots is a coach's dream, and, in all seriousness, it does not happen too often. Secondly, the defensive ends must be divided during teaching sessions so that they may learn

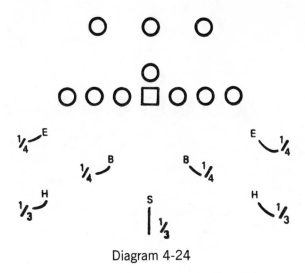

Diagram 4-24

The pass-prevention unit in 4-4-3 defenses.

how to read running keys as well as passing keys, and the reactions
that go with them. Thirdly, considering the fact that most high school
football teams are run oriented, the defensive ends should be more
pressure conscious; yet in this defense they can not be overly aggressive on penetration. Another consideration is the type of passes
thrown and the distance of passes thrown in high school competition.
The type of pass is usually play-action or roll-out, and the distance of
the passes, in general, never exceeds twelve yards. For these additional reasons, we feel that the 3-deep defense is weak against the run
around the ends, and extremely weak against play-action or roll-out
passes in the short areas. The defense is excellent for the team that
believes in multiple sets up front, but these variations could be nullified by attacking weak areas that remain constant.

THE 5-3 DEFENSE

Many of the advantages of the 4-4 defense prevail in the 5-3
alignment, and the weakness at the defensive end area is compen-
sated for by the presence of aggressive, penetrating defensive ends.
Variations in the alignment of the run-prevention corps can be
utilized through stunts rather than positioning changes. Diagrams
4-25 through 4-28 show how the 5-3 can be varied and Diagram 4-29
how the pass-prevention unit works.

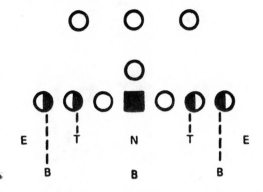

Diagram 4-25: 5-3 In Defense.

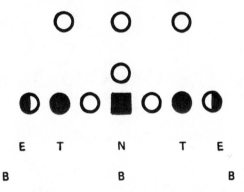

Diagram 4-26: 5-3 Out Defense.

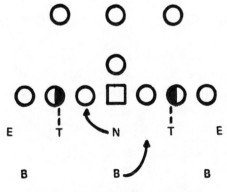

Diagram 4-27: 5-3 In Red Dog.

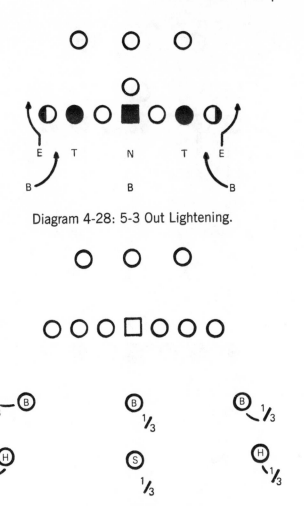

Diagram 4-28: 5-3 Out Lightening.

Diagram 4-29: The 5-3 Defensive Pass Unit.

This defensive set allows for a strong pass rush and strength off tackle and at the ends. The defensive pass zones are well covered although the under zones are only covered by three linebackers. Teams will employ the 5-3 defense to accomplish the following:

1. Five man rush vs. all passes.

2. Eight man run-prevention unit.

3. 3-deep pass defense with no rotation responsibilities.

4. Very easy to coach and to find personnel to man the positions.

The weaknesses are as follows:

1. Line stunts must be kept at a minimum since there is only one linebacker inside.

2. The middle is weak against dives and counters.

3. Play-action off-tackle with quick, short passes will hurt the "in" alignment. (See Diagram 4-30.)

4. Off-tackle power plays will hurt the "out" linebacker alignment. (See Diagram 4-31).

THE 6-2 DEFENSES

There is little distinction to be made between the responsibilities of the 4-4 defenses and those of the 6-2 alignments. The difference is

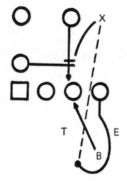

Diagram 4-30

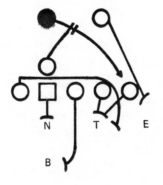

Diagram 4-31

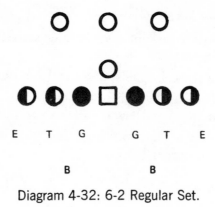

Diagram 4-32: 6-2 Regular Set.

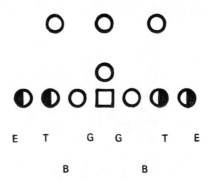

Diagram 4-33: 6-2 Short Yardage.

that with the 6-2 defense, the defensive ends may be more aggressive and only have pass responsibility on special situations. Furthermore, the pass-prevention unit may be involved in man-for-man coverage instead of the standard zone coverage. This frees the defensive ends for run-prevention only and it makes the ends tougher to run against. Some alignments are similar to the 4-4 sets, but there are variations. (Diagrams 4-32 and 4-33.)

The 6-2 alignment may be varied so that only one of the defensive ends has pass responsibility on wide-out offensive sets. In Diagram 4-34, the defensive end to the split end's side drops off the line of scrimmage and plays in the flat. If a running play develops, he will react like an outside linebacker; if a pass develops, he will be responsible for the 1/4 flat zone. The remaining defensive secondary and

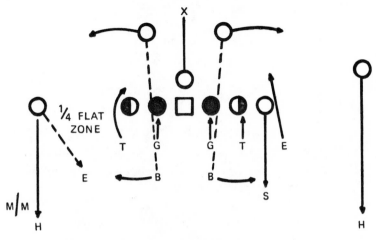

Diagram 4-34

The 6-2 defense showing pass-prevention with
man-for-man responsibilities, and the run contain
unit's rushing lanes.

linebackers are man-for-man conscious, while in the event of a running play, there are still eight men defending against it. (See Diagram 4-34.)

SHORT YARDAGE AND GOAL LINE DEFENSES

While there are some basic defensive alignments that are suitable for short yardage and goal line situations only, many such defenses originate from one or more combinations of the alignments already presented. Furthermore, the defensive pass coverage philosophy may vary by coach and not by alignment, for short yardage and goal line defenses lend themselves to either man-for-man or zone coverage without alteration in position. The classical characteristic of short yardage and goal line defenses is that there are only two lines of defense as opposed to the three lines of defense used by defenses in the open field. Diagrams 4-35, 4-36, and 4-37 depict the more popular defenses used in tight situations.

These defenses are used primarily in situations when the run is the expected offensive weapon. The defense tries to outnumber the offensive blockers so that at least one defensive lineman will be un-

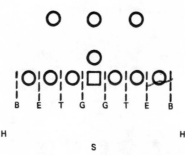

Diagram 4-35: The Gap 8.

Eight defensive linemen in each offensive gap. Primarily used against the run; easily adapted to man-for-man pass coverage.

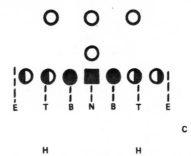

Diagram 4-36: The 7-4 Box.

The run is defended by seven men while the pass play may be covered by either a rotating zone or man-for-man.

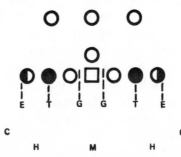

Diagram 4-37: The 6-5 Defense.

The most recent development in short yardage and goal line defensive alignments—because it can be used anywhere on the field. It lends itself to stunts, man-for-man and zone pass defense, and it utilizes a middle linebacker, unlike the other defenses for tight situations.

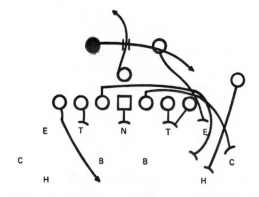

Diagram 4-38: Off-Tackle Power Play vs. 5-2
Defense.

Note the relative ease with which blocking assignments can be executed. Both guards are to
lead the play off-tackle; wingback blocks inside;
and all interior linemen block away from the point
of attack in order to seal off pursuit from the inside. In the open field and against this defensive
set, all blocking appears to be sound and consistent.

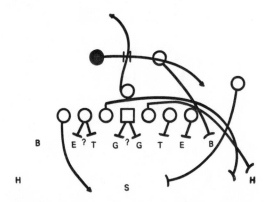

Diagram 4-39: Same Play vs. Gap 8 Defense.

In this short yardage or goal line situation, the
blocking rules must be varied or the play is
doomed to failure. Note how the pulling guards
have left both their center and tackle with a
dilemma—which man do they block? The only way
to run this play against this defense is to keep one
of the guards in or have a set of special short yardage blocking rules.

blocked. Furthermore, teams that run many of their power plays with pulling guards or tackles must reorganize their blocking rules for short yardage defenses, especially against the gap 8 alignment. Diagrams 4-38 and 4-39 illustrate how a typical off-tackle power play can be successful against a strong open field defense, but how it can also be broken down against a short-yardage defense such as the gap 8.

Realizing full well the problems that can be caused by short yardage and goal line defenses, the offensive line coach must prepare his blockers for this challenge. There are several ways that the advantages of these varying defensive alignments can be nullified, and we will attempt to cover some of the most basic and consistent ways, and also some of the more sophisticated ways for doing so in the next two chapters.

chapter 5

Simple and Consistent Rule Blocking

Having been introduced to the many variations a defensive team can come up with, the coach must next ask, "How can my linemen block these variations with any degree of consistency?" This question can be answered in many different ways, and throughout this chapter we will offer the reader what we consider to be the best possible way to block multiple defenses. This is not to say, however, that other ways of blocking are not both simple and consistent. Our system was developed with several things in mind, and it is because of these considerations that we find our system to be simple and consistent. The main considerations are:

1. Rules eliminate the need for combination blocks. Therefore, coaching time is reduced.
2. No opponent is restricted to one alignment per game; expect a change on every play.
3. Never expect the defender to wait; anticipate movement from every defender and beat him off the line.

Finally, we treat our rules as priorities, meaning that if the blocker considers one rule first and it does not apply to the situation, then he will rely on his second rule or priority, and so on. As the chapter progresses, the reader will see how we accomodate such defensive variations as stacks, slants and other stunts. But, as in any introduction, we must learn terminology . . .

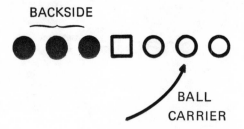

Diagram 5-1

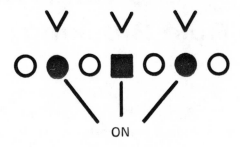

Diagram 5-2

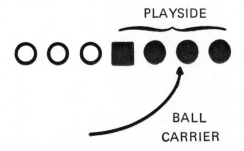

Diagram 5-3

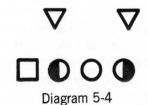

Diagram 5-4

TERMINOLOGY

In order for your linemen to understand what you expect of them, you must develop a common language. Coaches today are very conscious of ways of expressing football so that they can be understood by their players and by other coaches. The following terms should be learned by all offensive linemen before they attempt to learn their blocking rules.

Backside: Refers to that part of the line of scrimmage farthest away from the point of attack. We also refer to offensive linemen who are beyond the center and away from the point of attack as, "backside linemen."

Example: If the play goes to any point on the right of center, the left guard, left tackle and left end are all "backside." (See Diagram 5-1.)

Gap: Refers to the area between offensive blockers. Thus, the area between guard and tackle split is the guard/tackle gap, and the area between the tackle-end split is the tackle/end gap, and so on.

On: Refers to that defender who plays directly in front of the blocker. (See Diagram 5-2.)

Over: Refers to that defender who plays directly in front of the blocker, but off the line of scrimmage. In all cases, this term refers to a linebacker.

Playside: The opposite of backside. That side of the offensive line closest to where the ball is being run. This includes the center, guard, tackle, and tight end when used as "playside" linemen.

Example: If a play is designed to go to the right, then the center, right guard, right tackle, and right end are all considered playside linemen. (See Diagram 5-3.)

Point of Attack (P.O.A.): Refers to the exact area where the ball carrier is assigned to run. Many teams refer to the point of attack as the hole.

Shaded: This term refers to the position of the defender that puts him on the blocker's inside or outside shoulder. (See Diagram 5-4.)

Slant: Refers to a defensive maneuver whereby two things may happen:

1. A defender who is "on" will slant to a gap.
2. A defender who is aligned in a gap will slant to a position "on" a blocker. (See Diagrams 5-5, 5-6.)

Example 1.

Diagram 5-5

Example 2.

Diagram 5-6

Special Plays: Refers to any play where one or more linemen are required to pull out of their normal position. Specific play-types would be traps, powers and sweeps.

Stack: Name given to a defensive alignment where two defenders occupy the same area, one directly behind the other. The stack may occur in the on position or the gap position. (See Diagram 5-7, 5-8.)

Straight Plays: Refers to any play other than those that are "special." No lineman will pull out of the line and all blocking will be basically "straight."

Inside: This term applies to the position of the center of our offensive line. If we say "inside gap," the implications are different for each lineman. Diagram 5-9 shows the blocking pattern as it would look if the linemen were to block to their "inside gap."

BLOCKING RULES FOR STRAIGHT PLAYS

As the definition above states, straight plays are those which require only straight ahead blocking. Specific play-types would be dives, slants, sneaks, and options. In none of these plays do we attempt to block the defenders at the ends or corners. Any play that we want to attack these areas uses special blocking, e.g., pulling line-

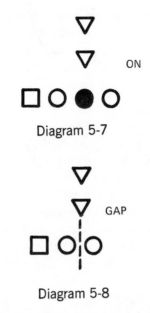

Diagram 5-7

Diagram 5-8

Diagram 5-9

men. Therefore, with this in mind we can set up our blocking patterns without concerning ourselves with the wide defenders. Our rules for these straight plays are as follows:

1. Block the defender playing in the on position.
2. If no defender is in the on position, block the defender in the over position.
3. If no defender is on and no defender is over, then block the defender in the playside gap.
4. If no defender is on, over, or in playside gap, then block backside areas.

As the reader will quickly see, these rules are presented in terms of priorities. They attempt to cover every possible alignment the defense can assume near the blocker. Naturally, we do not require that our linemen learn these rules in such a long, and verbose style, we abbreviate the rules to read as follows: "For any straight play, block the man on, over, playside gap, or backside." It is imperative that each blocker think in that order.

PRACTICAL APPLICATIONS

In the subsequent diagrams we will show how these simple rules can accomodate a multitude of defensive alignments for the same play and thereby demonstrate the consistency of this rule system. For the sake of the diagrams, we will use the following hole numbering system as a source of reference. These holes are, in effect, our points of attack, and we demand that every linemen know the location of every point of attack relevant to his own position. This goes along with the requirement that every lineman know the terminology perfectly. (See Diagram 5-10.)

The first play (Diagram 5-11) will be a simple dive play through the 1 hole against several defensive sets. Remember that the rules are: on, over, playside gap, and then backside.

Now let's take the same basic play and run it against an odd defensive alignment. Note how our priorities accommodate this defense. (See Diagram 5-12.)

Now that we have diagrammed an offensive line with hole numbers, the word "playside" has significant meaning, for now the linemen who are nearest the point of attack know exactly where the ball is being run. The advantage of this type of numbering and priority blocking has a tremendous value in goal line situations, for there is no need for a special set of goal line blocking rules. In the diagrams that follow, several points may be attacked with powerful blocking that more than accommodates the gap 8 defense, a defense used very often in short yardage and goal line situations. (See Diagrams 5-13, 5-14.)

These few examples show how consistent the rules can be for open field defenses and short yardage defenses. Now we will take a look at the more sophisticated stacked defenses.

RULE BLOCKING VS. STACKED DEFENSES

Stacked defenses pose the greatest problem for a team's blocking rules simply because most rules depend on the alignment of the

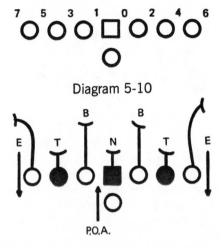

Diagram 5-10

Diagram 5-11: Dive Through the 1 Hole vs. 5-2
Regular.

1. Both ends have resorted to their last priority:
   backside.
2. Both tackles are blocking according to their first
   rule: on.
3. Both guards block their second priority: over.
4. The center blocks the man on.

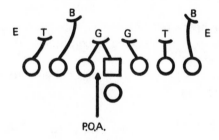

Diagram 5-12

1. Left guard and center block according to their
   third priority: playside gap.
2. Left tackle and left end also block playside
   since neither of them has a man on or over.
3. Right tackle blocks man on, his first priority.
4. Right end has no man on, so he blocks second
   priority which is man over.

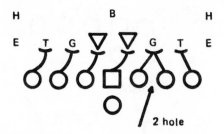

Diagram 5-13: A 2 Hole Play vs. the Gap 8.

1. None of the blockers has a defender on or over, so each man is blocking playside.
2. We get an automatic double-team block at the 2 hole.

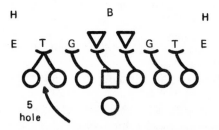

Diagram 5-14: A 5 Hole Play vs. the Gap 8.

1. None of the blockers have a man on or over, so each man is blocking according to his third priority, playside.
2. Again, we get an automatic double-team block at the 5 hole.

defenders before the ball is put into play. In reality, the stack alignment does its work after the ball is snapped, and unless the blockers know what to expect from the stack in front of them, confusion sets in. Stacked defenses do not pose a great problem for our rules because we take the time to teach the theoretical use of stacks, and we block according to those possibilities. Diagram 5-15 shows two different ways that an on stack can stunt against the offense.

When the stack is on as in Diagram 5-15, the offensive lineman must assume that some sort of stunt is in the making. Very seldom will a stacked alignment remain stationary after the ball is put into play. By virtue of the on position, we contend that the only effective

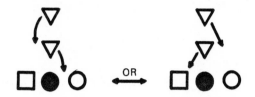

Diagram 5-15: The Stacked Defense On Position.

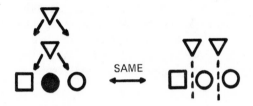

Diagram 5-16

We consider the on stack to be the same as a gap
defense.

slant will be when the defenders attack the gaps on either side of the
blocker. It is possible for them to slant over to the center's nose or
over to the tackle's nose, but I doubt that this distance could be
covered effectively. Thus, any blocker who sees a stack on him, automatically assumes that on the snap of the ball at least one of the
defenders will be in his inside gap and one will be in his outside gap.
The right tackle is also aware of the possible outcome of the stack that
is on his guard. He anticipates that on the snap of the ball there will
be a defender in his inside gap. And finally, the center too is aware of
the stack on the guard. He assumes that on the snap of the ball one of
the defenders will be in the gap between himself and the right guard.
In effect, the gap set up we have diagrammed is blocked or attacked
with our priorities the same way as a gap defense would be. (See
Diagram 5-16.)

The next diagram shows the blocking pattern in accordance with
our rules for the on stack as compared to the gap defense. (See Diagram 5-17.)

A second way that a stacked alignment may be used against the
offense is in the gap between two blockers. Several common gap
stacks appear in Diagrams 5-18, 5-19, 5-20.

The gap stack again has two possible ways of slanting. The

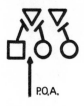

P.O.A.

P.O.A.

Diagram 5-17

1. Right guard must block the man on, according to his first rule.
2. The right tackle assumes that a man will end up in his inside gap, and he is blocking according to his third priority: playside.
3. The center blocks according to his third rule also since there is no defender on or over.
4. The result is similar to the blocking pattern against the gap defense.

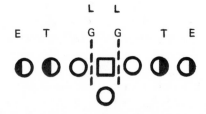

Diagram 5-18: Center-Guard Gap Stack.

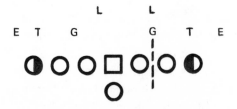

Diagram 5-19: Guard-Tackle Gap Stack.

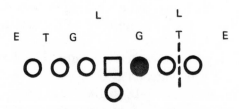

Diagram 5-20: Tackle-End Gap Stack.

linebacker can slant right while the lineman slants left, or vice versa. What we assume is that the slant maneuver from the "gap stack" will be attacking the nose of the two blockers involved. In other words, if the stack is in the guard-tackle gap, these two linemen can expect to have a defender "on" them after the ball is snapped. The diagram depicts what we expect the defense to do. (See Diagram 5-21.)

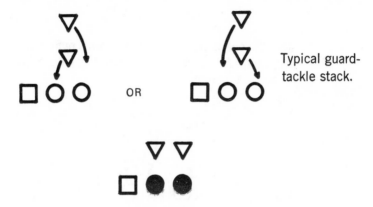

Typical guard-tackle stack.

This is the actual way we assume the gap stack will end up.

Diagram 5-21

Since this type of stack could result in a stunt where one defender attacks the guard and the other attacks the tackle, both linemen must assume that they will have a man on them at the snap of the ball. It does not matter which defender slants into which blocker, both men must block according to their first priority against the gap stack, i.e., block the man "on". In order to insure that the blockers make the correct initial step to stop the penetration of the man in the gap, we refer back to our step drill. Both the tackle and the guard will step directly towards the man in the gap. Once the stacked pair of defenders makes its move, then the blockers can pick up their one-on-one assignments. If the stack does not split, then we get a double-team block by the guard and tackle on the defensive lineman in the gap. Diagrams 5-22, 5-23, 5-24 show how the blocking pattern forms. (See Diagrams 5-22, 5-23, 5-24.)

It should be obvious that we could block the stacked defensive alignments with special types of blocking, such as the cross-blocking

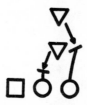

Diagram 5-22

Both the guard and tackle step towards man in the
gap; guard picks up inside charger, tackle picks
up outside charger.

Diagram 5-23

Same step results in guard still picking up inside
charger and tackle picking up outside man.

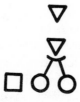

Diagram 5-24

The initial step puts both blockers in a position to
double-team the defender even with no stunt.

outlined in Chapter 2, but these simple rules should also prove that
elaborate and sophisticated techniques are not usually necessary if
you are willing to analyze the defense and take away its advantages
with sound one-on-one blocking and simple, consistent rules. The

diagrams that follow show blocking patterns against defenses using both types of stacks. Check for yourself to see whether or not the blocking rules are being observed by every lineman. (See Diagrams 5-25, 5-26, 5-27.)

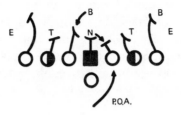

P.O.A. is the 0 hole.

Diagram 5-25: The 5-3 Stacked Defense.

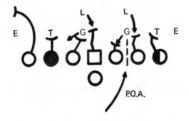

P.O.A. is the 2 hole.

Diagram 5-26: The 6-2 Gap Stack Defense.

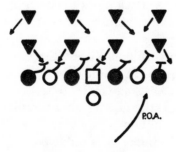

P.O.A. is the 4 hole.

Diagram 5-27: The 4-4 Stacked Defense.

BLOCKING RULES FOR SPECIAL PLAYS

In accordance with our terminology, special plays are those plays that require that one or more linemen pull out of the line to execute their block at the point of attack. In our system special plays are traps, sweeps, and pitch-outs. The blocking rules will vary slightly in plays of this type for the simple reason that on these plays, one or more of the interior linemen will not be in his regular position at the snap of the ball. The blocking rules for special plays are as follows:

Onside Linemen

    1. Check-block for the pulling lineman next to you.

    2. Block first gap away from the P.O.A.

    3. Block the man on.

    4. Block the man over.

    5. Block backside.

Backside Linemen

    Block exactly as you would for the "straight" plays, that is:

    1. On.

    2. Over.

    3. Playside gap.

    4. Backside.

The only change is in the blocking of the onside linemen because the special play makes a check block necessary (see Chapter 3). Diagrams 5-28 through 5-30 will illustrate the need for check blocking in a selection of special plays

With the additional rule and these three examples, we can now see how the blocking patterns would develop against specific defenses for special plays. (See Diagrams 5-31, 5-32.)

The reader should note how a rather complex play such as a trap, can be executed without complex rules. One simple change in the blocking of the onside linemen is sufficient to compensate for the pulling blocker.

Through careful study of our special plays and the various defensive sets, the rule change for onside linemen became necessary. It is a

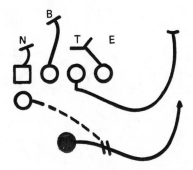

Diagram 5-28: The Pitch-Out.

The tight end will check block for the pulling tackle.

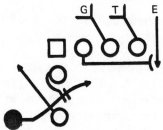

Diagram 5-29: The Trap.

The onside tackle and end must check block for the pulling guard.

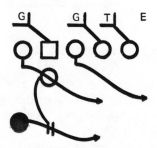

Diagram 5-30: The Sweep.

The center, tackle and end are check blocking for the pulling guards.

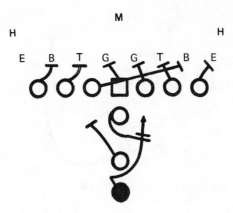

Diagram 5-31: The Trap at the 4 Hole vs. Gap 8.

1. Onside linemen block according to first priority: check block. Thus, center will check for pulling guard.
2. Right side of line then blocks according to second rule, i.e., block first gap away from P.O.A.
3. Backside linemen block according to their regular rules which has all of them blocking their third priority: playside.

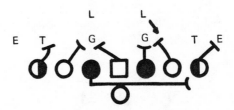

Diagram 5-32: Trap at the 4 Hole vs. 6-2 Stack.

1. Onside linemen are right end, tackle, guard and center. Each is blocking according to his first priority for a special play: "Block first gap away from the P.O.A."
2. Backside linemen are the left tackle and end, and they are blocking according to their third priority: playside; since no defender is on or over.

simple change and easy to remember. The one thing that helps line-men remember the difference between straight plays and special plays is the name of the play, such as dive, trap, sweep, counter, and so on. Coupled with the hole numbering system, the linemen are more than blockers, they become intelligent thinkers and are able to analyze the reasons for blocking for specific plays in specific ways.

ADVANTAGES

The summary of this introduction to rule blocking is best pre-sented in a list of the advantages of using such a system.

1. The consistency of the rules is guaranteed, since they are listed as priorities, not exceptions.
2. The rules can be used for all plays, straight as well as special, against all defenses, short yardage as well as open field.
3. The offensive line can use its rules against a defense it has never seen and still block it consistently.
4. Coaches can work longer on teaching fundamental blocking and not on teaching defensive alignments. All that needs to be learned are:
   a. Hole numbering.
   b. What play name means, i.e., straight or special.
   c. The blocking rules themselves.
5. The time required to teach this system is less than most others.
6. As a blocking system it may be used for any type of offense, wishbone, winged-T, pro-set, or unbalanced-line.
7. The rules encourage the linemen to seal off penetration by nature of the order of the priorities, and penetration can destroy the running game.
8. A defense that shifts, stacks or slants can not confuse the blockers who have learned this system.
9. Detailed scouting reports concerning the defensive aligments are not necessary. If scouts are difficult to come by, this is a tremendous advantage.
10. If in any particular season, good offensive linemen are scarce,

the straight blocking rules will accommodate weaknesses in the offensive line. Many teams are not blessed with the luxury of two fine pulling guards and they must therefore run all their plays with one-on-one blocking. This system is made for such a situation.

There are systems of blocking that teach the linemen to count the defensive personnel in order to find their assignments; there are systems of blocking that teach the linemen to block specific areas rather than specific men; there are systems of blocking that are different for every single play; and, finally there is the system that we offer here that combines every good aspect of all the other systems and adds simplicity and consistency to each and every offensive play. In the next chapter, we suggest a way to sophisticate these rules that might appeal to coaches who have the advantage of two-platoon players and can work with their offensive linemen daily.

chapter 6

The Call System
of Offensive Line Play

In this the final chapter pertaining to blocking techniques for the running game, we offer the reader a sophisticated method for blocking all defenses while at the same time utilizing the best possible block-type to accomplish the task. The types of blocks that will be involved in the calls are those that have already been discussed and taught; therefore, we will not elaborate on the techniques of each block again, but rather on the call system itself, it's usage and advantages. Call blocking is not new to all coaches, but it may very well be revolutionary when used in high school football. The reason for this statement is simply that we hope to convince all readers that this system can be implemented even in programs where two-platoon football is impossible. Since we advocate simplicity throughout our line play techniques, it is once again part and parcel of the "call system." As in the case of the rule-blocking we offered in Chapter 5, the call system requires that certain prerequisites be satisfied. The terminology offered in the next section provides the base for these prerequisites.

TERMINOLOGY

Thorough understanding as well as memorization of the following terms will facilitate learning the call system:

The Call-Men: Those offensive linemen responsible for calling the type of block to be used.

The Mike Call: The call that requires man-on-man blocking. (Man-on-man = mike.)

Fold Call: The call that requires a cross block with the outside lineman stepping first and the inside man going around behind.

Bingo Call: The call that requires a cross block with the inside man going first and the outside man stepping around behind.

Pinch Call: The call that requires a double-team block.

Wedge Call: The call that requires that two blockers converge on one defender, or on one area as in the case of a gap-stack.

THEORY

Theoretically, call blocking is another way of defeating the opponent who uses multiple defenses or makes drastic adjustments on the field. If the offense is successful in running a particular play off-tackle, it wants to be able to continue running this play no matter what defense is thrown up to defend against it. Since many plays now in use call for a specific type of block at the point of attack, teams that use multiple defensive alignments are able to adjust and prevent that blocking type. Consequently, the offense must either discard the play or take valuable time to adjust their blocking. Consider the off-tackle play diagrammed below. The play calls for a double-team block at the 4 hole and, as Diagram 6-1 clearly shows, the play will be successful against the 5-2 defense.

After giving up big yardage, the defense wises-up and makes a slight adjustment to their off-tackle position. The adjustment may be in the form of changing the 5-2 alignment to a wide-tackle alignment, as in Diagram 6-2. Note how this change eliminates any possibility of a double-team block at the point of attack.

An offensive team who's blocking rules are so fixed that any adjustment would require a time-out or even rejection of the play as in this example, could stand to learn the theory of the call system. With the call system a designated lineman at the point of attack would be able to call for a specific kind of a block when faced with a specific kind of a defense. In the case of the same off-tackle play vs. the 5-2 defense, the call man would call "pinch" in order to get the double-

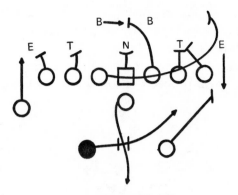

Diagram 6-1

Off-tackle power play vs. 5-2 defense with double-team block at the point of attack.

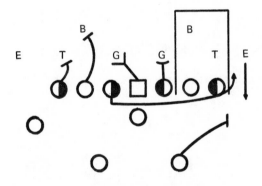

Diagram 6-2

The same off-tackle power play vs. wide-tackle adjustment. The double-team between tackle and end is taken away.

team block with his end. When the offense comes over the ball the next time to run the same play and the defense has switched to the wide-tackle setup, the call man now calls "mike," which tells the end that the double-team block is off and that man-on-man blocking will be used. This way the blocking is adjusted immediately at the line of scrimmage and the play can continue to be run against the ever changing alignments. In the diagrams that follow, the power play is run against three different defenses. Each time the call is changed at the line of scrimmage and the play is run at the same point of attack, but with blocking types that accommodate the defense. (See Diagrams 6-3, 6-4, 6-5.)

This concludes the explanation of the theory of the call style of blocking. Now we will proceed to the actual breakdown of how the system works.

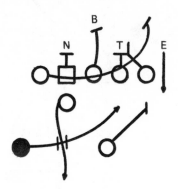

Diagram 6-3: Power Play vs. the 5-2 Defense.

The call between tackle and end is "pinch".

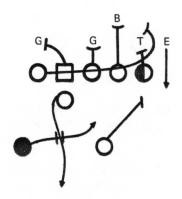

Diagram 6-4

The power play again, only this time against the wide-tackle defense. The call between tackle and end in this case is "mike," to get man-on-man blocking instead of the double-team.

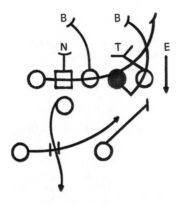

Diagram 6-5

Once again the power play is run to the 4 hole, this
time vs. the 5-3 stack. The call is "fold" so that
the tackle and end can pick up the stack and the
play is still sound.

HOW THE CALL SYSTEM WORKS

Two facets of the call system that are vital have already been
discussed. First, our blocking rules are called by the priority system
as outlined in Chapter 5. Second, the points of attack, or holes, are
numbered by gaps as shown in Diagram 6-6.

Although one might not think that this numbering system is
significant, in reality it is vital to the call system. The reason for this is
that any call that is made can only affect two blockers, and in order to
alert the two proper blockers, the point of attack must be between
them. As an example, see how Diagram 6-7 illustrates those linemen
who are near each hole. Clearly, if you name a point of attack, there
are always two linemen who know that they are right next to that
hole.

To emphasize the need for this numbering system, let's look at
another type of numbering system and see if we can accommodate the
call system theory with it. (See Diagram 6-8.)

This system numbers the linemen rather than the gaps, and the
confusion that comes in from this setup can be seen when we ask the
question, "What two blockers are near the 5 hole? The 2 hole? The 6
hole?" As you can see, if we were to run a play into the 6 hole for

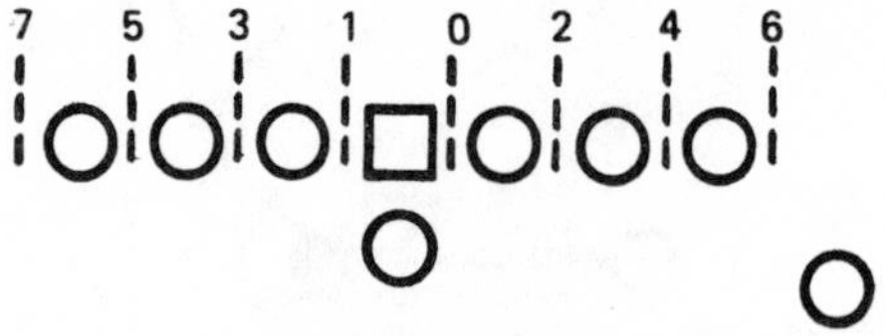

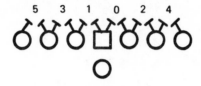

Diagram 6-6

Hole numbering system for call system.

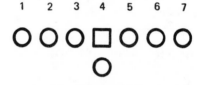

Diagram 6-7

Diagram 6-8

example, the right end, right tackle, and right guard are all near the hole. Thus, if a call was to be made to change the blocking, three men would have to be involved, and this would cause a great deal of confusion. I contend, therefore, that gap numbers are vital to this system, whether they are numbered in order or by evens and odds makes no difference.

DESIGNATING THE CALL MEN

The call men actually control the blocking from end to end on the offensive line. It is therefore imperative that we choose linemen who are located central to all points of attack. Through trial and error, we found that the tackles and the center would be able to call the blocking for every point of attack. Diagram 6-9 shows that the right tackle's call can be directed to himself and the right guard when a 2 hole play is called, and his call can be directed to himself and the right end when a 4 hole play is to be run.

The left tackle on the other side of the line has the same responsibility. His calls will control the left guard, himself, and the left end blocking patterns. Thus, plays run to the 3 and 5 holes can be blocked different ways by the left tackle's calls. (See Diagram 6-10.)

Finally, the 0 and 1 holes are controlled by the center. His calls will direct the right and left guard depending upon which hole is to be attacked. If the play being run is a 1 hole play, the center's call will be directed to himself and the left guard. (See Diagram 6-11.)

Diagram 6-9

The right tackle makes calls for the 2 and 4 holes, thus controlling the blocks of the right guard, himself, and the right end.

Diagram 6-10

The left tackle controls the blocking of the left end for 5 hole plays, and the blocking of the left guard for 3 hole plays.

Diagram 6-11

The center's calls change the blocking-types at the 1 hole for the left guard, and at the 0 hole for the right guard.

Up to this point we have the following essential ingredients for installing the call systems:

1. Terminology and code names for block-types.
2. A set of one-on-one blocking rules.
3. Theoretical reason for using this system.
4. A hole numbering system to accomodate call blocking.
5. Designated call men.

Now let's assume we are in a ball game and the opponent is using multiple defenses on every play.

GAME SITUATION

The quarterback calls a play in the huddle, "30 dive, on two." The team breaks the huddle and assumes the pre-set position. While in this pre-set position the three call men look over the defense and decide what call they want to make. Before the quarterback says "Down," a call is made by all three of the call men. The only call which has any meaning is the call made by the center, since he controls the blocking for the 0 hole. The call made by the two tackles are "dummy" calls. The dummy call is essential so that the defense can not pick them up and react to them. Dummy calls are made on every play, regardless of whether it is a pass, run or kicking situation. In Diagrams 6-12, 6-13, and 6-14, the 30 dive is shown with several blocking schemes against several defenses.

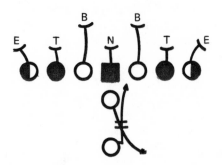

Diagram 6-12: 30 Dive vs. 5-2 Regular

Center calls "mike" for one-on-one blocking.

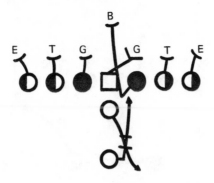

Diagram 6-13: 30 Dive vs. 6-1 Pro

Center calls "bingo" to get cross block with right guard.

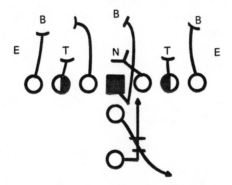

Diagram 6-14: 30 Dive vs. 5-3 In Defense

Center again calls for a cross block, only it is a fold technique that controls the 0 hole and right guard.

Since the calls that are made only affect the blocking that goes on at the point of attack, the other linemen simply block according to their rules. In each of the preceding diagrams, the linemen not involved in the call were blocking according to:

1. On
2. Over
3. Playside gap
4. Backside

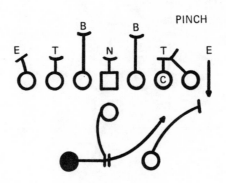

Diagram 6-15: 34 Slant vs. 5-2 Regular.

Tackle calls "pinch" to get double-team with his 4
hole partner, the right end.
All other linemen block according to their
priorities.

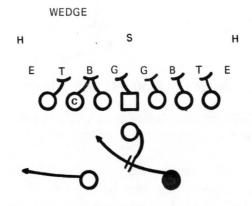

Diagram 6-16: 23 Quick vs. Gap 8.

Left tackle is the call man. He calls "wedge"
which gives him and the left guard a double-team
at the P.O.A. Note how every defender is blocked
by other blocker's use of priorities. Their third
priority is in effect, playside gap.

The beauty of the call system lies in the fact that while you are getting the best possible block at the point of attack to accommodate the ever changing defense, at the same time you are getting the most simple and consistent rule blocking everywhere else. This type of blocking system allows for sophistication as well as simplicity and consistency. Please take note of the application of the regular blocking rules executed by the blockers not involved in the call as well as the types of calls being used against defensive changes. (See Diagrams 6-15, 6-16.)

At this point, the reader should have some questions about the ability of the linemen to know what call to make. On paper it looks very good, but how does a high school lineman know the difference between using the mike and the pinch call? Or more difficult yet, the fold versus the bingo call? The next section will be devoted to answering this question.

HOW TO TEACH THE USE OF CALLS

In order to be a great offensive lineman, the player must understand defensive alignments, strategy, and techniques. Although it may not always be part of the coach's philosophy, we insist that every lineman learn a defensive as well as an offensive line position. Through some practical experience, insight into the actions of the defensive linemen is gained. The first process in teaching the way calls are to be used is to teach the offensive linemen how to recognize the defense in front of them. We break the multiple defenses into each blocker's position area and then show them what alignments are possible and what calls can be made. We never refer to a defense as odd or even, because we are only concerned with how the defense is aligned at the point of attack. Once the blockers learn the possible alignments, we show them how they are similar, and eventually, we categorize defensive alignments according to our blocking calls. For example, there is absolutely no difference between a 5-2 alignment and a 6-1 alignment over the center and right guard. All that has happened is that the linebacker who was over the guard in the 5-2, came down to an on position on the guard and the nose-guard in the 5-2 dropped back to a middle linebacker. Since this type of change does not affect the point of attack, say the 0 hole, the blocking type may be the same. The changes that are of major concern are those that move a defender from an on or over position, to a gap or stacked position. In the chart that follows, we have diagrammed the possible defensive alignments that the right tackle and right end will see, and the possible calls that could block these alignments. (See chart, Diagram 6-17.)

For further simplification, the reader should note that every defensive alignment, with the exception of the stacks, can be blocked with mike blocking. Therefore, if you wished to keep the calls to a minimum, you would merely teach your linemen to recognize stacked defenses and the calls that you want them to use for them.

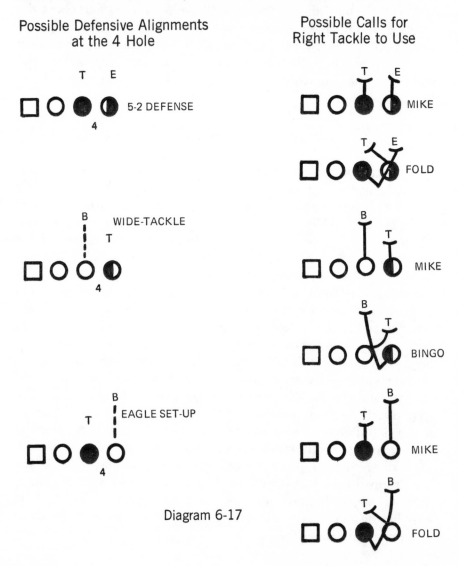

Possible Defensive Alignments
at the 4 Hole

Possible Calls for
Right Tackle to Use

Diagram 6-17

Possible Defensive Alignments
at the 4 Hole

Possible Calls for
Right Tackle to Use

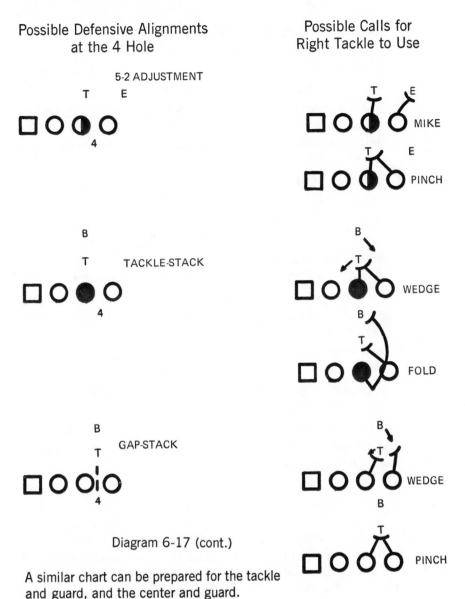

5-2 ADJUSTMENT

MIKE

PINCH

TACKLE-STACK

WEDGE

FOLD

GAP-STACK

WEDGE

Diagram 6-17 (cont.)

PINCH

A similar chart can be prepared for the tackle
and guard, and the center and guard.

ADVANTAGES OF THE CALL SYSTEM

As a final tribute to the call system, we offer the reader the
advantages of its use as we have found them in the past years:

1. It enables the offensive team to utilize the best possible

block at the point of attack on every play against every defensive alignment.

2. It teaches the linemen how to play football. They are no longer considered "stupid" linemen.

3. Scouting reports need not be so detailed, and if they are not detailed enough, the call system will still accommodate the defensive sets, even when the linemen have not been exposed to them previously.

4. Call blocking is an extra advantage that the blocker has over the defender.

5. It is the coach's answer to multiple defenses with a certain amount of sophistication, simplicity and consistency.

6. The complete offensive game plan may be used regardless of defensive adjustments. No plays need be discarded.

7. Memorization of what block-type is to be used for which play, is no longer necessary. The blockers will determine their own blocking.

8. Teaching time is cut to a minimum, leaving more time for the coach to perfect fundamental blocking techniques.

9. It allows for on-the-field adjustments to be made by those people closest to the situation.

10. It gives part of the game to the players, much like playcalling gives the game to the quarterback, consequently, player morale improves.

CONCLUDING REMARKS

The running game is the major part of high school football, and I dare say, as a phase of football, it has to be the most important part of the game. The running play sets up every other possibility in offensive football, and without a substantial running attack, the passing game will be sporadic to say the least. The techniques have been presented here in a cumulative manner, indicating that one precedes the other, and so, having established a sound running game, we proceed to put the ball in the air.

part III

How to Block
for the Passing Game

chapter 7

Drop-Back Pass Blocking

Drop-back passing is a vital part of every offensive system. Any coach who uses dropback passing must spend a great deal of time perfecting and disciplining his receivers on their pattern routes and his quarterback on his drop-back action as well as his ability to read defenses. In these two areas alone, the coach will spend at least half of his practice time. Yet blocking for this form of the passing game involves far more technique and requires far greater skill and talent than does running of pass route or catching the ball. Drop-back pass protection is an art, and as an art it demands precision, balance, agility, intelligence, technique, and an equal amount of practice time spent with receivers and quarterbacks. The techniques and coaching points offered in this chapter represent a compilation of over fifteen years of personal offensive line playing experience, and nine years of offensive line coaching experience. Any coach who has searched for teaching aids in this area of the game or who has looked for special techniques that will afford him the best pass protection possible, would do well to read and re-read this chapter.

A PASSING PHILOSOPHY

The team that uses the drop-back pass as an offensive weapon must also have a particular philosophy about the passing game. By "philosophy" we also mean "reason," the question, "Why do we drop-back in order to throw the football?" must be answered. We use the drop-back pass sparingly, but we have definite reasons for using it at all, and we find that those reasons also support our philosophy on the overall passing game.

First, the formation changes that are made to accommodate the receivers in their execution of pass patterns for a multitude of routes can also help disguise your running game. For example, if you split an end and a flanker whenever you want to drop-back and pass, this will spread out the defensive secondary. By spreading the defense with a passing formation, you make all your running plays more threatening since the secondary must defend against the wide receivers first and often lose sight of their interior keys. Because of this, it follows that our particular philosophy would favor the running game first, while using the drop-back passing attack as a complement to it. Many other coaches tend to follow the opposite philosophy, which places primary importance on the passing game while using the running play as a change-up.

Second, by passing from the drop-back action from a number of different formations, you may force the defensive secondary into a variation of its normal coverages, which leads it to confusion. Once this begins to happen, you can make the job easier for the passer because he will be able to pick up weaknesses in the coverage and isolate one primary target. This reduces the possibility for interceptions or quarterback sacks.

Third, the variations in formations automatically provide your offensive running game with the multiplicity that confounds the line and linebackers, which in turn makes your offensive linemen's jobs easier.

Finally, in the event that a drop-back pass is absolutely necessary, say for instance in a two-minute drill at the end of the half or at the end of the game, the bomb becomes more effective since the defense is merely guessing at what you are going to do when your team sets up over the ball. Whatever your philosophy is on the passing game, the coaching techniques employed by all involved must never be shortchanged, regardless of whether you throw four times per game or forty-four times per game. If each pass is to be executed properly, then these are the techniques that should be taught . . .

THE STANCE

As in the running game, the stance becomes the first major technique that will determine whether or not the block will be well executed. In no way should the stance be altered to accommodate pass blocking but must remain the same as that stance used in all situations. Offensive linemen should be taught to respect their defensive counterparts enough never to cheat in their stances, for any good defender will pickup that change and read the play every time. Drop-back pass blocking is one technique that will certainly tell whether or not the blocker has a perfect stance. When blocking for the running play, a blocker would not be hampered by a stance that caused him to have his weight too far forward, but should he keep this stance in an attempt to pass block, he would be in deep trouble. The stance should be such that the weight is perfectly balanced so that the blocker can move in any direction with maximum quickness, power, and balance.

THE TWO-POINT STANCE

The very best position to start from in drop-back pass blocking is the two-point stance. But, since we seldom if ever ask our linemen to block straight ahead from this position, this statement may seem contradictory. There are definite advantages to the two-point stance in pass blocking, and before we explain the contradiction, we should point out the advantages of the two-point stance. First, in this stance the blocker's head and eyes are up and he is afforded maximum visibility. In cases when drop-back passing is imminent and the defense is stunting, looping, or blitzing in some way, visibility is vital. Second, the blocker does not have to set himself in a balanced position on the snap of the ball, he is already up and prepared to make contact in a good hitting position. Third, this two-point stance gives the blocker more time to see how the defender is charging without back peddling right away. If the defender charges to the inside, the most dangerous route as far as the blocker is concerned, then the blocker is already prepared to protect this route. Finally, this stance practically eliminates those embarrassing times when a quick defender out-charges your blocker and knocks him over on his backside while your blocker is attempting to set up to pass block.

DISGUISING THE DROP-BACK PASS

One might wonder about the contradiction here: Doesn't the two-point stance give away the fact that we are going to pass? The answer is no. Furthermore, it will add to the disguise of the drop-back pass if used when the offensive team breaks the huddle and the offensive linemen set themselves in a pre-set position, i.e., the two-point stance. This is done prior to every play, regardless of whether it is run or pass. On most occasions, the quarterback will make signal calls, a set call, or even a check-off call, but on some call the linemen would get down into their offensive stance. However, once the defense men get used to this routine, they will not actually prepare themselves to rush or stunt or loop, or do whatever it is they have planned to do, until the linemen are in their three-point stance. Therefore, when we are going to throw a drop-back pass, we will snap the ball on the quarterback's first sound while the linemen are still in their pre-set stance. By doing this we feel we give ourselves the following advantages:

1. It puts the blocker in perfect pass protection posture instantly.

2. Defensive maneuvers in the line are negated by the offense's quick start. The defense loses the element of surprise.

3. Due to the quickness of the snap, the defense loses it's quickness so vital in pass rushing.

It is imperative that the blocker never tip-off the defender by any variation in the way he pre-sets himself on each and every play, run or pass. The quarterback's cadence must also remain the same and with a consistent rhythm and sequence. In this way, the two-point stance will never give a drop-back pass away to the defense, and at the same time it will give the blocker the best possible advantage over the defender.

THE CORRECT INITIAL STEP

Before any lineman can become an effective pass blocker, he must be fully aware of the many defensive tactics that are available to his opponent. Once aware of the defensive tactics for pass rushing, the blocker can prepare himself and use some techniques of his own to protect the passer. The first tactic used by many defensive pass rushers is a slanting charge to the inside of the blocker. This path is the shortest route the defender can take and it becomes the most dangerous to the blocker. The inside route must be taken away from the defender immediately. This can be accomplished very easily by teaching the pass blocker to take one simple step each and every time he blocks for a drop-back pass.

On the quarterback's signal to put the ball in play, each and every offensive linemen must take a lateral jabstep towards the inside. This initial step must be lateral and not backward, as a backward step will create a gap between the two neighboring linemen. Also, this initial step need not be any more than six to eight inches as it is merely a position step. If this initial step is taken quickly and correctly, it will discourage the defender from shooting to the inside and it will force him either to run straight ahead or take the outside route. In either case, the blocker has taken the inside path away from the defender and forced him to go where he can be blocked the way the blocker wishes. The blocking scheme showing the initial step as it should be taken by the interior linemen is shown in Diagram 7-1.

The technique is completed when the blocker sets his other foot. Having completed the inside jab-step which is a position step, the blocker now drops his outside foot back on an angle of forty-five degrees with the line of scrimmage. Thus completed, the initial step cuts off the inside route and actually "suckers" the defender into charging to the outside. All this technique is accomplished with little or no contact between the blocker and the defender. The total picture of the initial step is seen in Diagrams 7-1 through 7-3.

The offensive center represents the middle-man in the formation of the pass protection unit, and as such he does not need either the jab-step or the drop-step technique in dropback passing blocking. His

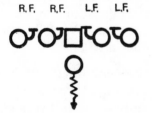

Diagram 7-1: The Jab Step (Phase 1).

Initial step to the inside.

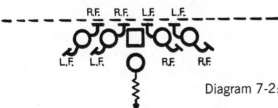

Diagram 7-2: Phase 2.

The jab-step and drop-step combined.

Diagram 7-3: Phase 3.

The protection cup formed by initial step.

initial steps must first get him into the correct two-point stance for balance and all-around blocking posture. The center's snap should be of sufficient force as to enable him to get up into a hitting position quickly. From here he will drop-step straight back or as the defender playing over him dictates. This blocker should keep his shoulders parallel with the line of scrimmage for as long as possible before looking to either side for a man to block lest a linebacker loop up the middle on a blitz. The next phase of the drop-back pass block involves the keys. These are the fundamentals of drop-back pass blocking.

THE FUNDAMENTALS OF DROP-BACK PASS BLOCKING

It goes without saying that the first and foremost fundamental is a sound blocking stance, and this has already been described as the two-point stance. The second fundamental has also been described and that is getting into the proper position to begin blocking the defender. Having accomplished this much, the blocker must now be prepared to make contact with the defender and keep him away from the quarterback without going downfield past the neutral zone. We can best teach the reader these techniques in the same way we teach our assistant coaches and the players themselves. We will list each technique and then add a full description for each one:

1. *Foot-fire.* In order to maintain the proper hitting position and absolute balance throughout contact, the blocker must keep his feet moving constantly from the time the ball is snapped until the time the play is blown dead. We refer to this action of the feet as foot-fire and we emphasize it constantly. The athlete must move his feet rapidly about shoulder width, on the balls of his feet, and with short choppy motions. As soon as this action stops, the athlete will instinctively lean or lunge at the defender and fall to his knees. Foot-fire, when executed properly, insures that the blocker will remain on his feet throughout all contact made with the defender.

2. *Clench fists and hands high.* We combine these two techniques because they both involve the hands. Clenching the fists insures that the blocker will not grab the defender and be guilty of holding. By keeping the hands high, we stress the use of hands and forearms as a shield against the blows delivered by the defender. Much in the same way that a boxer will use his hands and arms to parry the blows delivered by his opponent, the pass blocker should keep his hands and arms high to parry the hand and arm tactics used by the defender. These techniques include side shots to the shoulder and head area of the blocker, which, if delivered with enough force, could knock the blocker off balance. By anticipating these blows and defending against them, the blocker can maintain his balance and continue to be an effective part of the pass protection unit. The blocker must remember that while he may use his hands and arms to protect himself, he may not use them to stop a defender from passing him or to keep a defender away from his body. This would be illegal use of hands and arms and warrants a fifteen yard penalty.

3. *Use proper contact surface.* The proper surface with which the blocker should make contact with the pass rusher is generally determined by the nature of the pass play, but for drop-back action we insist that the blocker keep the defender right in front of him. Contact can then only be made with the shoulder and the fists. The type of contact sustained in pass blocking is relatively free of the same kind of force one encounters in one-on-one blocking for the running game. Furthermore, the eyes are nothing more than an aiming or sighting device that helps the blocker keep the defensive man in front of him. We also advocate the use of the fists' instead of the forearms as a point of contact. With the eyes and fists the blocker should meet the charging defender and make contact with him about chest high. The fists are better than the forearms as a point of contact in that they enable the blocker to get a quicker and better feel for the way the defender changes the path of his charge toward the quarterback. If the pass rusher hits the blocker straight on and then slides quickly to the right, the blocker will feel the extra pressure on his fist and will be able to react properly more quickly than if he used his forearms as a contact surface. It should be noted however,

that if the blocker uses his fists to prevent the pass rusher from getting past him, or if he overextends his fists, he will again be guilty of holding. The proper technique for using the fists requires only that the blocker keep his elbows close to his body and the fists up close to his chest.

4. *Hit-retreat-chop!* The passer requires at least seven seconds for a normal drop-back pass, and in order to get this kind of time, the blocker should avoid trying to maintain constant contact with the defender. If he does try to maintain contact, he may be overrun, thrown to the side, or out maneuvered by some fancy footwork or hand tactic. To avoid this possibility, we teach a hit-retreat-chop tactic which gives us the necessary time for effective pass protection.

   a. *Hit.* In this phase, the blocker merely squares himself in front of the defender and hits him squarely in the middle of his chest. This hit is only forceful enough to stop the rusher's forward progress long enough for the blocker to get away from him and retreat.

   b. *Retreat.* The blocker quickly resets himself in a hitting position by retreating to avoid being grabbed or out-maneuvered by the defender. His retreat should be deep enough to get clearly away from the defender but not so deep that he interferes with the passer. The retreating action, along with the hitting action, must be accomplished with constant foot action or foot-fire technique.

   c. *Chop.* Once the blocker has retreated, enough time has elapsed so that the rusher must commit himself to one route. At this point the defender is hell-bent for the quarterback, and is probably at full speed. When this situation presents itself, I teach my blockers to chop the defender and take him cleanly off his feet. The chop block must be executed perfectly, or else the defender will recover and still make the play. To chop the defender, the blocker will keep his head up and his feet constantly firing in place, with no forward or backward movement. As the defender gets right on top of the blocker, the blocker throws his head to the outside and his shoulders into the rusher's thighs. This chopping action is intended to take the defender down completely, which also has the advantage of bringing his hands down so that he can't block the pass or the passer's vision by simply extending his hands.

The hit-retreat-chop technique may be altered in many ways. It may be shortened to simple chop-blocking, excellent for quick passes that require no time at all. Also, this technique may be extended to hit-retreat-hit-retreat-chop to insure that the blockers do not cut the defender too soon. In any case, we feel that the chop phase should be included in drop-back blocking techniques since it lends itself nicely to those linemen who are not exceptionally big or strong but are continually playing opposite bigger opponents. It is also a much easier way to learn pass blocking, since many high school programs do not have the time or the coaches to spend all kinds of time teaching pass protection of the quality used in professional football.

TYPES OF DROP-BACK PASS BLOCKING

There are three types of drop-back pass blocking styles that can be used. The coach may select one specific type and use it exclusively, or he may teach all three types and give his blockers the privilege of calling what type they will use as they discover the way the defenders put on the rush. The determining factors will be coaching time available, ability of the linemen, and overall passing philosophy. The first and most common type of drop-back pass protection is the cup protection and is outlined below along with man-for-man pass protection, and a more recent type that we call the slide technique.

CUP PROTECTION

This type of pass protection is perhaps the most common and the easiest to teach. Beyond the coaching of the jab- and drop-step techniques, cup protection requires little else in coaching. The main point to stress to the offensive blocker in this type of pass protection is that the defender must be kept to the outside of the middle zone where the quarterback is setting up to pass. Once the initial steps have been taken and the blocker has closed off the inside rushing lane, he may keep the defender outside in two ways:

1. *Aggressive blocking.* The blocker attacks the defender and may use any one of many one-on-one blocking techniques already described in Part I. Diagram 7-4 shows that the blocker is

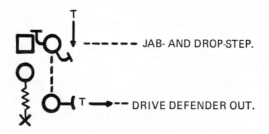

Diagram 7-4

Aggressive blocking for drop-back pass protection.

driving the defender away from the quarterback's zone and is in effect, blocking him as though it were a running play. The blocker in this type of protection actually "suckered" the defender into a position where he could be blocked from the side.

2. *Hit-retreat or shuffle technique.* The pass blocker again takes his initial steps to seal off the inside lane, but in order to keep the pass rusher outside, he will hit and retreat and continue to do this protecting the inside zone occupied by the passer. The blocker shuffles his feet laterally as he hits the defender and retreats, but his contact with the defender is only forceful enough to keep him from penetrating to the inside, not forceful enough to knock him down. As a last resort, the blocker may chop the rushers legs out from under him. Diagram 7-5 depicts the imaginary line along which the pass blocker must shuffle in order to keep the defender out of the passer's zone.

Cup protection has its greatest advantage when the two set-backs in the offensive formation join the blocking unit. This setup affords maximum pass protection as it accounts for all defenders on the line as well as any linebackers that may blitz. The disadvantage occurs when the offense wants to send more than three receivers out for a pass. When this occurs another type of pass protection should be used. Diagram 7-6 shows the formation of the entire blocking cup. Cup protection is based on area blocking philosophy, which simply means that if there is no defender in a given area, the blocker will have no responsibility other than to act as a helper or to beware of a blitzing linebacker. (See Diagram 7-7.)

Diagram 7-5

The inside position step forces the rusher to go outside the blocker. The blocker keeps the defender out of the passer's zone by shuffling, hitting and retreating gradually.

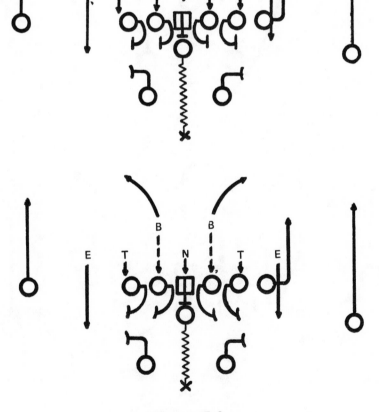

Diagram 7-6

Cup blocking scheme vs. two different defensive sets.

The disadvantage of cup blocking is clearly seen when a fourth receiver is put into the pattern. Note how the defensive left end has a clear shot at the passer. A different type of pass protection is needed here.

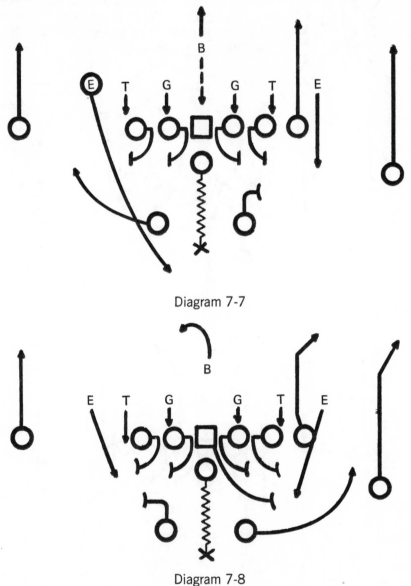

Diagram 7-7

Diagram 7-8

Center's pass block vs. even man defense with right halfback in the pass pattern. All assignments are man-for-man.

MAN-FOR-MAN PASS BLOCKING

Cup protection is a very conservative means by which dropback passing may be protected. In order to open up the options of receivers to throw to, and to sophisticate the passing game, coaches may go to the man-for-man protection. In this type of protection, each blocker is assigned a specific man, and he must block that man no matter where he goes. The rules for man-for-man protection would be as follows:

Center: Block the nose-guard in an odd defense; if no down lineman is playing head up on you, drop back and block the defensive end to your right or left. You will block left when the left halfback is in the pattern, and you will block right when the right halfback is in the pattern. Coach's play calling usually includes some key that tells the center which way to block. (See Diagram 7-8.)

Guards: The guards are responsible for the first down lineman to appear off the center. They are never responsible for the nose-guard, nor are they responsible for a blitzing linebacker as they were in the cup type of protection. (See Diagrams 7-9, 7-10.)

Tackles: The tackles are responsible for the second down lineman to show off the center. In both the odd and even defensive alignments they will be blocking the biggest, strongest and quickest lineman on the opposing team. Therefore, teams that use the man-for-man type of pass protection should select their offensive tackles keeping this in mind. (See Diagrams 7-11, 7-12.)

Man-for-man pass protection is best used against a defense that only uses four defensive linemen to rush the passer. As soon as the defense rushes more than four people, the offense must keep one or more backs in to help block. Blitzing is very effective against the team that employs man-for-man pass protection exclusively. It is very helpful to be able to send four or more receivers downfield in a passing situation, and in such a situation man-for-man pass protection is excellent. But to use this type exclusively would soon force the defense to blitz and stunt more often than normal, making your pass protection extremely weak. The final type of pass protection allows the linemen to make changes in their blocking on the line of scrimmage without affecting the backfield blocking or the kind of pass patterns that can be used. We call this "slide" blocking.

Diagram 7-9
Guards' man-for-man blocking assignments vs.
odd man defense.

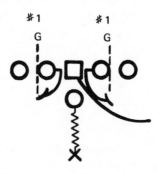

Diagram 7-10
Guards' man-for-man blocking assignments vs.
even man defense.

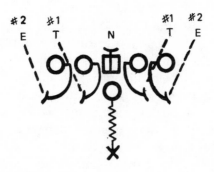

Diagram 7-11
Tackles' blocking assignments in man-for-man
protection vs. odd man defense.

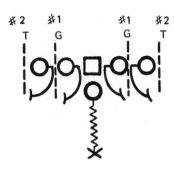

Diagram 7-12
Tackles' blocking assignments in man-for-man
protection vs. even man defense.

SLIDE BLOCKING FOR DROP-BACK PASSES

The act of sliding in this type of pass protection is done by the guards. They will slide down from their positions to the outside to pick up a rushing defender so long as no one has rushed over their regular positions. Before sliding to the outside, the guards will check to make certain that no linebacker is blitzing over them, for if one does blitz, the guard must block him. Using the slide technique gives you the advantages of both the cup and the man-for-man types of pass protection. On any particular pass play, one or both guards may slide, or it is possible that the defense will be such that neither guard can use the technique at all. Diagrams 7-13 and 7-14 show how and when the slide technique might be used in a number of defensive situations.

The offensive tackles will always block the man on or slightly to their outside. There is never any counting done with this type of pass protection, and it is designed to protect the middle first, the outside second. Middle blitzes should never hurt the passing game with this type of pass protection. The slide technique may also be used in the backfield. For example, if the right halfback is assigned to block the end, and the end drops off in pass defense, the halfback should then be able to slide off into the flat or hook zone for a short safety pass. (See Diagram 7-15.)

Coaches must consider every aspect of their offensive theory before choosing one of the three types of pass protection offered in this chapter. Regardless of which type of pass protection is chosen,

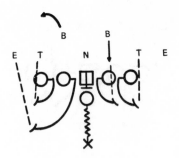

Diagram 7-13

Slide blocking vs. 52 defense with one linebacker blitzing.

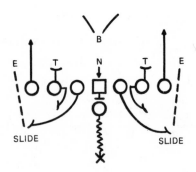

Diagram 7-14

Slide blocking vs. 53 defense.

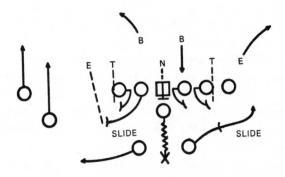

Diagram 7-15

there are certain fundamentals that are consistent. They are as fol-lows:

1. Coach the perfect stance and pass blocking posture.
2. Coach the correct initial step to close off the inside.
3. Coach the legal use of hands, clenched fists and hands high.
4. Coach foot-fire, the rapid and constant foot movement.
5. Coach hit-retreat-chop, a series of techniques.
6. Coach rules that make for easy assignments and easy reading.

With these simple coaching points and the techniques offered here, you will see vast improvements in the overall drop-back passing game, with fewer interceptions and fewer quarterback sacks. In the following two chapters we offer some fine techniques that will enhance the effectiveness of your air attack while faking the running game.

chapter 8

Sprint-Out Pass Blocking

When a team predominantly throws the football by dropping back, the defense can regulate its coverage and challenge the offense to execute properly. There is very little surprise involved in an offense that drops back each and every time it is going to throw the football. Furthermore, the coverage techniques for the defense are relatively simple against the straight drop-back passer since the defense has only to mirror the drop-back depth with its own drop-back. On the other hand, should the offensive team sprint-out to one side or another before throwing the football, the defense has to rotate towards that side as well as drop-back for depth, and these two movements often leave gaping holes in the coverage zones. It is also relatively easy for the offensive team to incorporate several running plays off the sprint-out action, making coverage even more difficult for the secondary. The great advantages of sprint-out passing are enhanced when an offense employs drop-back passing as well, for these combinations keep the defense confused and uncertain as to whether it should rotate or drop back, cover pass or defend against the run. In the pages that follow we will give the reader the best possible techniques for blocking on the sprint-out pass.

A PASSING PHILOSOPHY

The reasons that support the "why" of the sprint-out pass are many. Since the passer must sprint to one side or another, the defense must rotate quickly so that he will not get outside the coverage zones. Moreover, as the passer sprints-out, he takes the passing pocket with him and thereby forces the entire defensive secondary to move with him. This rapid rotation forces the secondary to vacate the side away from the direction of the sprint-out. Passes, screens, or draws that go back to this side are quite deadly for this reason. Another asset not found in any other style of passing is the quarterback's option to run as well as to throw. Many coaches call this type of pass a "run first—pass second" option since the secondary will more often than not hang back in expectation of the pass and leave the quarterback uncovered. The threats to the defense are many and, if more than two receivers are sent into an area on a "flood" pattern, the options are limitless. This type of passing game makes the running game more effective, while at the same time, there is not the same kind of a burden on the offensive linemen when it comes to blocking for the pass. The act of sprinting-out by the passer forces the pass rushers to go in one precise direction, and since the blockers already know which way the passer will sprint-out, they can expect the rushers to charge a specific way. The techniques of pass blocking become greatly simplified and position becomes the true key to successful sprint-out pass blocking. If your philosophy is predicated on the running game, then the sprint-out pass is an extremely good complement. Many coaches, however, will refrain from using the sprint-out pass for the simple reason that their quarterback is not a great runner. The quarterback need not be a 1000 yard gainer in order to make the sprint-out effective, but as long as he poses some threat as a running back, the defense will have to respect him. Thus, the philosophy that holds the running game in higher esteem than the long bomb or a predominant passing attack is maintained by the sprint-out pass.

THE STANCE

We can never say enough about the necessity for the proper stance in all phases of offensive line play, and the sprint-out pass is no different. However, unlike the drop-back pass that requires the blocker to drop-back as he makes contact with the defender, the sprint-out pass does not require a retreat. All that is required is that the blocker get good position on the pass rusher and influence him away from the quarterback's route. For this reason the blocker does not have to be set in a two-point stance but may move easily from his regular set position to a comfortable blocking posture. This is not to say that the same technique for starting a play in the pre-set position could not be used, for starting from the two-point stance would certainly not hamper the blocker. Thus, the quick count while blockers are still in their pre-set stance is still an effective surprise weapon.

DISGUISING THE SPRING-OUT PASS

Because it is difficult to throw a long drop-back pass from a tight formation, many times a team will also split an end and spread out their intended receivers. The sprint-out pass, however, can be thrown from any formation, tight or spread, since the passer's sprint-out gives the receivers enough time to get well into their pass routes. Since tight formations are often associated with running plays, this would be one way to disguise a sprint-out pass. Another way is to use men in motion, something not often used in drop-back passes. The men in motion may be used as blockers for the sprint-out passer, as decoys for the running game, or they may be used as safety valves in the actual pass pattern. Greater still as a disguise is the very nature of the sprint-out itself. Since the passer can either run or throw the ball, the options make it possible for the sprint-out to be used at all times, for long yardage as well as short, inside the opponent's ten yard line or inside your own, on first down or on fourth. The greatest disguise is the sprint-out game itself. Finally, since the offensive linemen do not have to retreat to block as in the cup or man-for-man styles of drop-back passing, the defensive secondary is unable to read their keys quickly enough to successfully defend all the options that are open to the sprint-out team.

THE CORRECT INITIAL STEPS

The initial steps taken by the offensive linemen reflect the same steps taken by the passer on his sprint-out route. If the passer is to sprint-out to the right, he must step with his right foot first and in the intended direction. Since this action will draw the defenders to the right also, it is essential that the offensive linemen anticipate this step and move in that direction as quickly as possible. Everyone on the offense knows which way the sprint-out will go and their initial steps will put them in the best possible position to meet the defender. Furthermore, the defense's reaction to the direction of the sprint-out is not immediate, and if the offense takes its initial position step properly, it will have a tremendous blocking angle on the pass rushers. The direction of the sprint-out sets the stage for the initial steps taken by each blocking lineman. The linemen are then divided into two categories, the onside linemen and the backside linemen. If the sprint-out is left, the onside linemen are the center, left guard, and left tackle, while the backside linemen are the right guard and the right tackle. If the sprint-out is to the right, then the center, right guard, and right tackle are considered onside, while the left guard and the left tackle are backside. The distinction must be made here because after the initial step is taken, the interior linemen will block with different techniques depending on whether they are onside or backside linemen. These techniques are the basic fundamentals of the sprint-out pass block.

THE FUNDAMENTALS OF SPRINT-OUT PASS BLOCKING

When a forward pass is thrown, certain rules govern the behavior of the interior linemen which prohibits them from going beyond the neutral zone. Violation of this rule makes the lineman guilty of a fifteen yard penalty as an ineligible receiver. When a quarterback decides to run the football after seeing that a drop-back pass will not be successful, the linemen will often cross the neutral zone and go downfield to block for the scrambling quarterback. Since nothing but pass was planned in the huddle, the quarterback's decision to run catches everyone off guard and may result in a big gain or, should the quarterback decide to pass afterall, it may result in an ineligible receiver downfield in the form of an overzealous lineman. The very nature of the sprint-out pass allows for the option of running or passing without the possibility of an ineligible receiver. Let's say that the sprint-out is to the right. In this case, the offensive linemen will all take a position step and drop-step to the right to get position on the defender. The onside linemen, center, right guard, and right tackle, will block aggressively without retreating and in the same manner as an area block. Since they are onside, they know that the quarterback will sprint past them quickly and that a quick, aggressive block is all that is needed so that the quarterback may get past the defenders on that side of the line. After taking their position step, it would be perfectly fitting for the onside blockers to chop the defender, because the sprint-out goes so fast that they could never hope to recover in time to stop the play. The idea of area blocking by the onside linemen will also negate any attempt made by the defense to blitz or penetrate towards the side of the sprint-out. In the diagrams that follow, onside blocking is shown as it may accommodate several different defensive tactics. (See Diagrams 8-1 through 8-3.)

The sprint-out pass requires an aggressive block at the corner as

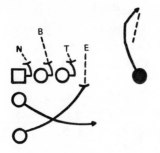

Diagram 8-1

Sprint-out right vs. 52 defense with blitz by onside linebacker.

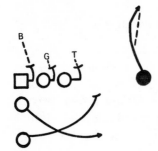

Diagram 8-2

Sprint-out right vs. 44 defense with onside linebacker blitz.

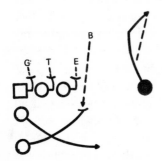

Diagram 8-3

Sprint-out right vs. gap 8 defense and outside blitz.

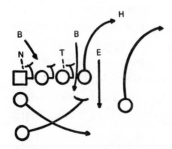

Diagram 8-4

53 defense with double blitzing puts great pressure on the passer.

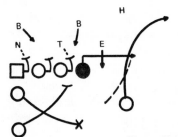

Diagram 8-5

The offense adjusts the tight end's pattern for quick pass in flat. The passer may also adjust his sprint-out and set up to throw rather than throw on the run. Line and fullback blocking remains the same.

indicated by the block of the fullback in the above diagrams. This block may be accomplished in many ways, but the most effective block is the threat of a running play. No fake between quarterback and fullback is necessary as long as there is some sort of running play established with this play-action. Although the onside linemen take a position step to the same side of the sprint-out, they are limited in their assignment to block only the defender on their outside shoulder. If a defender lines up on the tight end, for example, the onside tackle is not responsible for blocking that far to the outside. He will simply take his position steps and block the area head-on him and to his inside. The blocker who is responsible for the corner, in this case the fullback, is assigned to block the first man to appear outside his onside tackle. If more than one defender crosses the outside corner in an effort to put more pressure on the passer, then the sprint-out may be altered or a quick receiver may be added, both of which have the effect of forcing the defense to drop one man off for pass defense. Diagram 8-4 shows a defensive move to stop the sprint-out to the tight end side, while Diagram 8-5 shows how the offense would counteract this without changing the offensive line rules.

If an extra blocker were needed at the onside corner, a man in motion would be brought over and in some cases be used as a blocker or as a third receiver to flood the zones.

BACKSIDE BLOCKING

The backside refers to that part of the interior line away from the direction of the sprint-out. If the sprint-out goes right, then the left guard and left tackle are termed backside. The blocking techniques of the backside are different, for defenders attacking from this side are approaching the passer unseen by him, and more time is required to block these pass rushers. The technique for the backside linemen is simply the cup type of drop-back protection outlined in Chapter 7. Remember that cup protection is also area type blocking and should account for blitzing as well as regular defensive tactics. The backside linemen will still take their initial jab-step towards the side of the sprint-out, but unlike the onside linemen, their second step is a drop-step on a forty-five degree angle with the line of scrimmage. Once this position is taken, the backside blockers will protect their inside area first and from there, they will block any defender coming head-on them or slightly to their outside. If more than two defenders put the rush on from the backside area, the outermost rushers will go unblocked, for they are entirely too far away from the passer to make the play. Diagrams 8-6 through 8-8 show several defenses and how the backside linemen would pick them up.

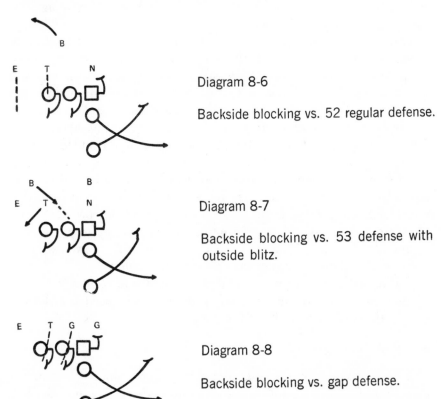

Diagram 8-6

Backside blocking vs. 52 regular defense.

Diagram 8-7

Backside blocking vs. 53 defense with outside blitz.

Diagram 8-8

Backside blocking vs. gap defense.

The backside linemen may use any one of the three types of drop-back pass protection techniques to block on the sprint-out. Backside blocking using these techniques is less dangerous than drop-back passing, because the passer's pocket gets further away with each second the rusher is delayed. For this reason, a lineman does not have to be a great pass blocker as long as he has been taught enough ways to stop or slow down the charging lineman coming from the backside. Again, the act of hitting, retreating, and finally chopping the defender makes for very effective pass protection on the backside of the sprint-out. Diagrams 8-9 and 8-10 that follow depict several ways that the backside linemen may block for the sprint-out passer.

The basics of blocking for any pass, whether it is a drop-back pass, a sprint-out pass, or any form of pass, should never change. Balance, position and foot-fire are always vital to effective pass blocking.

VARIATIONS IN SPRINT-OUT BLOCKING

The blocking patterns offered above are the simplest ways to block effectively for the sprint-out pass, but this does not imply that they are the only ways. There are a multitude of blocking schemes that will accommodate your sprint-out pass as well as your running game, and we will demonstrate several of these more sophisticated

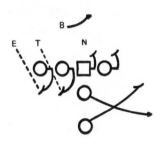

Diagram 8-9

Backside linemen using man-for-man type protection.

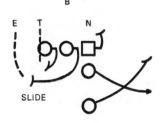

Diagram 8-10

Backside linemen using the slide technique of pass protection.

blocking schemes in this selection. In many cases, the major change is centered around the blocking of the defender who attacks the quarterback at the corner. As previously indicated, this defender may be blocked by one or more of the offensive backs. However, it is also a popular maneuver to block the corner with a pulling guard. In Diagram 8-11, the onside guard pulls to block the defensive end. The onside tackle and end block down to stop penetration and the fullback slants through the opening and flares into the short flat zone. A perfect complement to this pass play is the short trap diagrammed in 8-12.

The backside linemen are of course still able to block according to regular drop-back techniques, there would be no change for them in a situation like this. However, it is also possible to block the backside differently and disguise the sprint out pass with another sound running play. Diagram 8-13 shows how the common sweep play, with its two pulling linemen, can be alerted to fit a sprint-out philosophy. Diagram 8-14 maps out the blocking patterns for the line that will give the defensive secondary false keys and add to the surprise of the sprint-out pass.

No matter how you decide to vary the pattern of blocking for the sprint-out game, several things must always be considered as of the prime importance:

1. Block the sprint-out corner as strongly as possible.
2. Use whatever type of blocking consistent with your philosophy on passing. Do not burden your blockers with a multitude of techniques.
3. Protect the inside lines of pursuit to the quarterback primarily; then worry about the outside lines.
4. When the sprint-out pass is defended or stopped, adjust patterns or style of sprint-out; do not adjust or change interior line rules.
5. Use a variety of sprint-out blocking patterns to confuse secondary and defenders at the corner.
6. Use the sprint-out series to run, throw short, throw deep, run reverse and/or counters, screens and draws.

One particular series from our own sprint-out game is offered here as an example of item #6. In this series we were able to do a variety of things that no opponent ever stopped completely. (See Diagrams 8-15 through 8-22.)

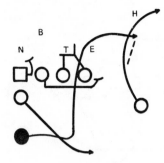

Diagram 8-11

Onside guard blocks at the corner while tight end and tackle block solidly. The fullback flares in short flat.

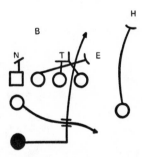

Diagram 8-12

A perfect complement to the sprint-out series would be this short trap off-tackle with fullback carrying.

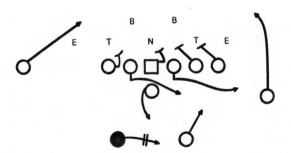

Diagram 8-13:
The Sweep Play.

Both guards lead the play, quarterback rolls into sprint-out route.

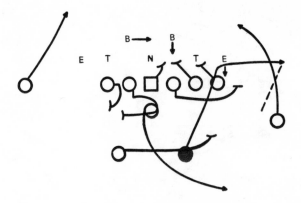

Diagram 8-14: The Sweep Action Sprint-Out Pass.

Lead guard blocks the corner, and trail guard peels back to protect the backside.

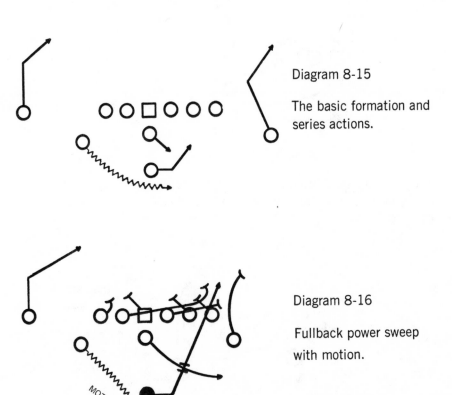

Diagram 8-15

The basic formation and series actions.

Diagram 8-16

Fullback power sweep with motion.

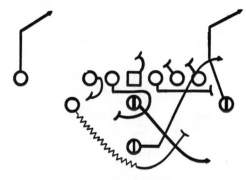

Diagram 8-17

Sprint-out right; quarterback has a run/pass option. The motion back helps guard block at the corner.

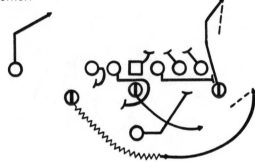

Diagram 8-18

Sprint-out right, with fullback and motion back switching assignments. Run/pass option again for the quarterback.

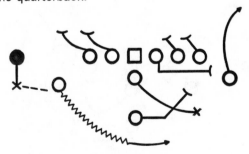

Diagram 8-19

Sprint-out right with quick screen throwback. Quarterback must set before throwing.

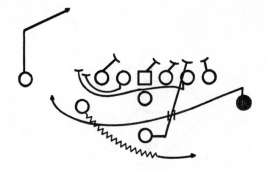

Diagram 8-20

Sprint-out right, wingback reverse. May also be run inside as a draw or trap. Good against teams that shift with motion.

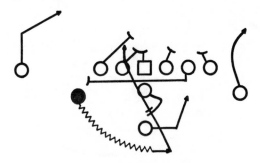

Diagram 8-21

Sprint-out right, counter-trap to slot back in motion. Very effective against teams that shift with motion.

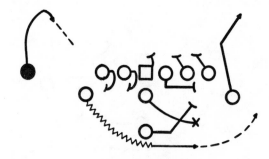

Diagram 8-22

Sprint-out right, throw-back to the split end. This receiver will simply find the open area and come back to the ball.

To make this series even more effective, we can put the wing in motion and run the sprint-out series to the split end's side. Greater variations can be added if the defense does not put great pressure on the corner and you can block that area with only one blocker. If this is possible, then patterns with as many as five receivers are available. Any defense that can stop all the options of the sprint-out series would truly be a well-prepared and well-disciplined opponent, and extremely difficult to beat.

chapter 9

Play-Action Pass Blocking

The play-action pass is the third and final type of pass that we will discuss in this section on the passing game. Its position in this part of the book does not reflect its importance. Quite the contrary; play-action passes are often the heart and soul of the passing attacks of many high school and college football teams, and they are dangerously effective weapons for a team with any kind of a running game. The play-action pass can be used for deception as a change-up for a powerful running attack, or it may be used as a surprise attack after a sudden turnover. More often than not, play-action passes are thrown under twelve yards in depth, and when they are kept short, the percentage of completion increases, making them an effective ball-control weapon. The play-action pass is also excellent for the team with less than average sized linemen or teams with a less than average throwing quarterback. Because of the necessity of backfield faking, the play-action pass is not conducive to use in a two-minute drill, the way the dropback and sprint-out passes are. However, the multiplicity of play-action passes far surpasses either of the other two forms of the passing game. Once the blocking skills for the running game and the drop-back passing game have been taught, pass blocking for play-action passes becomes second nature.

A PASSING PHILOSOPHY

We must have reasons for whatever we do, for the heart of successful coaching is preparation meeting opportunity, not luck. It is therefore proper to state reasons why the playaction pass should be incorporated into your offensive passing attack. The list is endless, but several reasons stand out and are worth explaining:

1. *As a complement to the running game.* If your offense is effective on the ground, averaging three or more yards per play, then chances are very good that a pass off the same type of play-action will also be successful. In this instance the defense has been drawn in closer by a repetition of successful running plays, amounting to a wide open secondary.

2. *For the benefit of inferior personnel.* If your quarterback is not too tall and can not throw very deep; if your line is relatively small and not too strong; and, if your receivers are not too fast and even a little short, you will never be able to throw a successful drop-back pass. The play-action pass provides the line great blocking angles, the quarterback wide open zones, and the receivers are usually wide open on short patterns. The quality of your athletes should determine whether or not you use this type of pass, but some play-action passes should be used by all teams at one time or another. The innate talents of your ball players will determine just how much you use play-action passes.

3. *To pass on first or second downs.* If you were to check the statistics of high school football games, you would probably find that over ninety percent of all first and second down plays are running plays. If you have a successful running game, why not throw from play-action on first and second downs? We try to anticipate the defense's train of thought, and whenever possible, unload with the unexpected. This kind of philosophy works especially well after your team has crossed the opponent's forty yard line, but the pass should be a short, high percentage pass.

4. *To surprise the defense after a sudden turn-over.* You have just recovered your opponent's fumble inside his own thirty yard line. He expects a run on first down, the game is a hard fought tie, what do you call? In our opinion, a play-action pass with two receivers, one deep and one short, would be excellent. The defense is probably very dejected over its mistake and will not be alert for the unexpected. Furthermore, should you fail to complete the pass, and even if it gets intercepted,

the opponent will not have gained much and you have the possibility of a quick score.

5. *To help the sprint-out passing game.* Because of the lack of a fake to a back in the sprint-out pass, the defense may rotate very quickly and shut down the passing lanes. If you add a play-action fake and then run the sprint-out action, the defense will be entirely too late in its rotation to stop the play.

In the long run, play-action passes help reduce the amount of coaching that must go into the season's preparation, for any number of plays may be taught, and then without much extra coaching, the same plays can be turned into passes. The line will simply have to be taught the proper ways to block for play-action passes.

THE STANCE

Since we want the defense to think "run," we must show them every offensive sign we can that a run is coming. To this end we have the cadence, formation and stance on every play-action pass accommodate this philosophy. We don't feel that an offensive blocker can get a good charge from a two-point stance for the running game, so, unlike the drop-back and the sprint-out pass, we would never start a play-action pass from the quick count or the pre-set stance. Every play-action pass will start from the perfect three-point stance, or whichever stance is considered the normal set position in your offense. As indicated earlier, we never retreat in play-action passes, therefore, a well-balanced, three-point stance is a must for the more aggressive blocking that benefits play-action passes.

DISGUISING THE PLAY-ACTION PASS

As the name implies, this type of pass is disguised by the action of the backfield. The backs will go through their normal routes for the makings of a particular running play. Since many younger players habitually key the running backs, this makes for a very effective disguise. Even more effective is the use of two or more wide receivers or motion backs when running play-action passes. These particular extras added to the color of the pass play force the defensive backs to focus their attention even more so on the backs or on the wide receivers, or even on the man in motion. This point is illustrated in the following diagrams where a number of offensive sets are used to run the same play-action pass. (See Diagrams 9-1 through 9-3.)

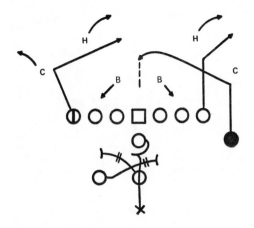

Diagram 9-1

Scissors action-pass that delays the linebackers' pass defense and leaves the middle zone area free. A secondary receiver may be sent deeper.

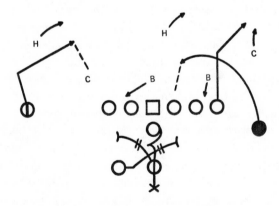

Diagram 9-2

The same backfield action with the added attraction of two wide receivers. The secondary must spread itself out more and still try to react to the running play. This makes open lanes greater and allows more time for deeper patterns.

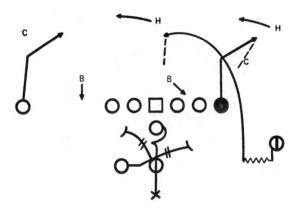

Diagram 9-3

The same backfield action with a man-in-motion.
This technique forces the defense to rotate out of
position while the receivers find the vacated areas.

So far the disguises we have described pertain to the backfield
action, but these disguises can be lost if the offensive line doesn't
disguise its blocking techniques also. A simple comparison will prove
my point. In the drop-back pass, the blockers must setup and drop-
step to get a sound blocking position on the pass rusher. Furthermore, since the rules forbid interior linemen to go past the line of
scrimmage on passes, the secondary can key on the line's footwork
and read that a pass is coming almost immediately. The sprint-out
pass takes a little more pressure off the offense and makes key-reading
more difficult, but since some of the blockers have to drop-back to
protect the passer, again the disguise is incomplete. On the other
hand, play-action passes are not only characterized by backfield faking, but the initial move of every linemen reflects the same move they
would make if the play were a run. Consequently, if the defensive
secondary is geared to key only the backfield, or only the offensive
line, they will be in deep trouble trying to stop play-action passes.
This initial movement by the blockers is not vital to the success of the
overall block, but it is vital to the disguise of the play-action pass.

THE INITIAL STEP

The initial step in play-action pass blocking boils down to an
aggressive step similar to the step taken in blocking for the actual
running play. To accommodate the rules that go along with the pass-

ing game, the linemen must avoid going downfield during the play, and this calls for special techniques that will be described shortly. The initial step can best be controlled by the blocking rules that go along with running plays with slight variations. Consider the following example: the blocking rules for the running game are given as priorities. That is, for all plays, the blocking rules for interior linemen are:

1. Block inside gap first.

2. Block man head on second.

3. Block outside gap third.

Use these same rules for blocking play-action passes and the correct initial steps will follow. The priority rules listed above are diagrammed for a particular play-action pass in 9-4. Note how the initial steps of the pass blocking unit resemble run-action. This technique helps disguise the play.

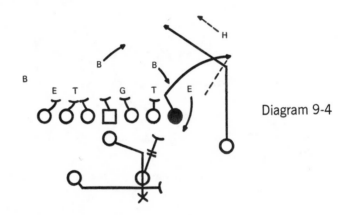

Diagram 9-4

Some highly successful offenses, such as the triple option wishbone offense, and the twin veer offense, predicate their play-action passes on the exact same blocking rules as the running game. In this way, the teaching of extra techniques is kept at a minimum while deception is kept at a maximum. Thus, whatever your blocking rules tell your linemen to do on running plays should also guide them in their initial steps on play-action pass blocking. The pairs of diagrams that follow show simple running plays coupled with an effective play-action pass, both of which show the same initial steps taken by the interior linemen. (See Diagrams 9-5 through 9-8.)

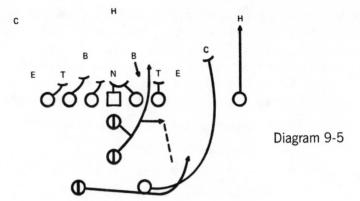

Diagram 9-5

The triple-option from the wishbone formation.

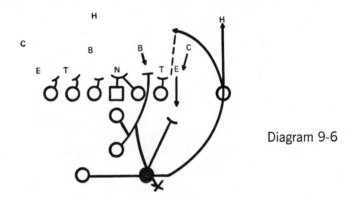

Diagram 9-6

The triple-option pass from the wishbone formation.

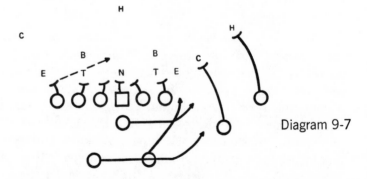

Diagram 9-7

The triple-option from the twin veer setup.

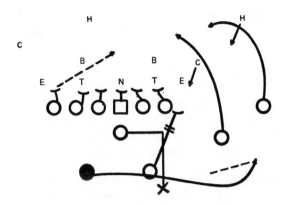

The swing or screen pass from triple-option action.

Diagram 9-8

AGGRESSIVE BLOCKING

There are a great many coaching books about the passing game, and when the author refers to play-action passes and the blocking that goes with it, he will always advocate aggressive blocking. What is aggressive blocking? Isn't all blocking supposed to be aggressive? Clarification is needed in an effort to understand this term. What writers are trying to distinguish is the difference between drop-back pass blocking, which allows the pass rusher to come to the blocker, and play-action pass blocking which requires that the blocker attack the defender. We don't want our players to think that aggressive blocking is only a part of play-action passes, but we do want them to know the different techniques required in various passing styles. The blocker must understand that his job in play-action pass protection is not only to prevent the defender from getting to the passer, but also to make the pass look like a run. To that end he must fire-out on the snap and attack the defender with 100% aggressiveness, never for a moment fearing that his aggressiveness will make him an ineligible receiver.

THE PROPER BLOCK

We have laid the foundation for a successful play-action pass:

1. The philosophy and reasoning is sound.
2. The disguises are built into the offense.
3. The blocking rules are consistent with the running game.

Now all that is left is a simple, consistent technique that will allow the blocker to be aggressive without the fear of crossing the neutral zone and becoming ineligible. Our advice is to use a block that will permit the blocker to make solid contact that can be maintained for several seconds and that will enable the blocker to turn the defender laterally down the line of scrimmage so that he can execute his block without ever crossing the line of scrimmage. We therefore teach all our offensive linemen the techniques of the following blocks used in one-on-one blocking (refer to Part I for full details):

1. *The scramble block.* As described in Chapter 1, the scramble block demands that the blocker get a quick start off the line, that he make good initial contact, that he accelerate on contact with the defender, and that he turn the defender away from the action laterally down the line. This type of block is especially good when the defender is in a head-on position, and has a size and strength advantage.

2. *The cartwheel block.* The blocker may well use this technique to show the aggressive attitude necessary to fool the defense, but at the same time, no forward driving is required. Once good contact is made as in the initial phase of a scramble block, the blocker will cartwheel his hips 180 degrees around the defender to prevent him from pursuit. An excellent follow-through for the cartwheel block is the technique called "crabbing" that helps the blocker move the defender laterally down the line.

3. *The hook block.* Defenders who align on the outside gap or outside shoulder of the blocker may pose a slight problem unless the techniques of hook blocking are perfected. In reality, the hook block only requires a quick jab-step for position, and then it becomes nothing more than a scramble block or a cartwheel block depending upon how contact is maintained.

Regardless of the blocking technique used, the fundamentals of stance, initial step, balance, foot-fire, and technique must always be perfect. These three blocking types will do some important things for your linemen when blocking for the play-action pass:

1. An aggressive attack at the defender.

2. Maximum contact surface.

3. Low position on the defender to prevent him from raising his hands and blocking the pass.

4. The ability to block for several seconds without crossing the neutral zone.

5. Disguising the pass to slow down pass rush and secondary's reaction.

UNCOVERED LINEMEN

The uncovered lineman can not go after a linebacker the way he would for a running play. However, the fact that he does not have a defender on or near him does not eliminate him from using any of the play-action pass blocking techniques just described. He must still fire-out quickly in a low position and attack the unmanned area closest to the normal blocking area he would be responsible for on a running play. He makes this move to continue the disguise of the play and as an anticipation of a slant or blitz that may come into this uncovered area. The typical example of such a case is against the stacked or tandem defense. In the situation diagrammed in 9-9, the right guard must anticipate that the middle linebacker and the nose-guard will be dealing, and therefore, he attacks the area the same way he would for the running game. If the stunt does materialize, the guard is ready, if not, then he will help the nearest lineman in a two-on-one situation. (See Diagram 9-9.)

PULLING LINEMEN

Some of the best plays in football are off-tackle power plays, traps, and sweeps. A common characteristic of these types of plays is that a lineman is pulled out of the line and assigned to block at the point of attack so that the offensive blockers will outnumber the defenders. If a team is successful running these types of plays, the defense will soon begin keying solely on these pulling linemen. When this happens, the offensive team can throw a play-action pass from the fake power, or the fake trap, or the fake sweep. But, in order for this

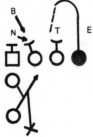

Diagram 9-9
Right guard's step vs. 53 stack on play-action pass protection.

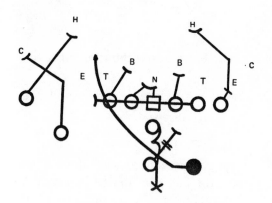

Diagram 9-10

Scissors play with trapping action.

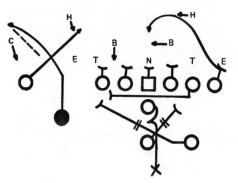

Diagram 9-11

Scissors pass with same trapping action.

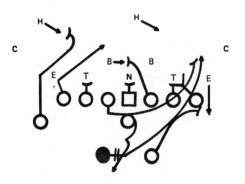

Diagram 9-12

Typical power play off-tackle.

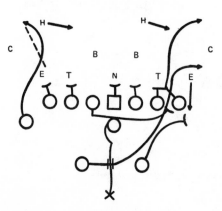

Diagram 9-13

Same power play action for play-action pass.

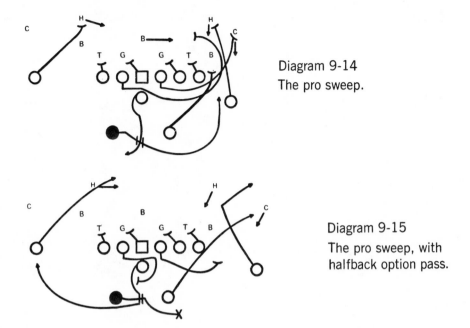

Diagram 9-14
The pro sweep.

Diagram 9-15
The pro sweep, with
halfback option pass.

type of pass to be devastating, the interior linemen must still execute their pulling blocks. It is perfectly suitable for play-action pass blocking to pull a lineman out of the line and have him block just as he would for the running play, because in power blocks, or traps, or sweeps, the lineman can show aggressiveness, make good contact, and still avoid crossing the neutral zone. Once the pulling lineman gets to the point of attack, he may use either the scramble block, the cartwheel block, or the hook block, judging from how the initial contact is made. If it happens that the defender does not penetrate, then the pulling blocker will simply pass-block at the assigned area the same way he would for drop-back or sprint-out protection. It is imperative, of course, that the backfield action remain the same and that the other blockers show aggressiveness and continue to block according to their rules for the running game. The diagrams that follow depict several very successful running plays and their complementary passes. The general flow of the blocking linemen give the defense the impression of "run" while the receivers are able to get open in their pass routes. Oftentimes, plays of this nature result in big gainers after the ball is caught. (See Diagrams 9-10 through 9-15.)

part IV

How to Block
for All Phases
of the Kicking Game

chapter 10

Blocking for Punts
and Quick-Kicks

If one looks at offensive football analytically, one may arrive at the following thoughts:

1. The offensive team has four chances or "down" situations with which they must move the football at least ten yards. In so doing the offensive team retains possession of the ball and gets another four downs for another ten yards.

2. Statistics show that the first and second downs are predominantly used for variations of the running game.

3. Unless the offensive team makes the ten yards in two plays, or unless the third down situation is for very short yardage, the offensive team will more than likely throw some form of forward pass on this down.

4. When the ten yard distance has not been negotiated after three attempts, the offensive team will punt the ball away to their opponents rather than risk going for the first down and missing it. In this decision, the coach has given up the football for better field position on his next possession. Coaches will make this decision at least 95 times out of 100 opportunities.

Judging from this, about the only sure thing the defensive team can count on is that on a fourth down situation with sufficient yardage left for a first down, that the offense will be punting. Furthermore, the offensive team must be prepared to punt the ball effectively if its reason for punting in the first place is to be justified. By giving up possession of the ball on fourth down, the coach assumes that his defense will do a good job and get him back the ball in better field position. In this way the punting game is actually being used as an offensive weapon, which we contend is the only way it should have to be used. The techniques and philosophy in this section of the book are based on several criteria:

1. The offensive team believes that the kicking down is still an offensive play and must be drilled the same as any running play or passing play.
2. The offensive team has a respectable punter who can average at least thirty yards per kick measured from the line of scrimmage, and a center who can snap the ball with maximum efficiency.
3. The offensive team has built up inside of itself a deep respect for every aspect of the kicking game, realizing that it can very well be the determining factor on foul-weather days, and in games against equally strong opposition.

The purpose of this chapter is to encourage a deep respect for the punting game with the hope that more time will be spent on this aspect of football within the allotted practice time. As indicated in the opening paragraph's analysis, in a series of four downs, the punt is used once, and on a tough day, it may be used twenty-five percent of the time. Can we, as coaches, afford to deprive our athletes of the necessary skills to make the kicking game win?

STANCE

Blocking for the punt is extremely similar to blocking for the drop-back pass, in fact, we make the analogy identical. As far as stance is concerned, then, all our punting is done from the two-point stance. This position gives the blocker great visibility, an important asset in punt blocking since many defenses will vary their alignment drastically for the sole purpose of blocking the punt or getting down-field to a particular zone. Consequently, the blocker will see alignments that he has never seen before on running or passing situations. Starting from the two-point stance gives him the advantage of seeing how the defense is set up and deciding where his priority block will be. Some defensive alignments against punt formations are heavy over-shifts or maximum blitzes, and the priority system of blocking for these multiple defenses is a must.

CADENCE

Unlike the running game, we believe in absolutely no sound at all for the snap of the ball on the punting situation. There are several reasons for this:

1. Since the blocker can not go downfield too soon anyway, there is no need for a quick start.

2. A pre-determined signal might put too much pressure on the center, forcing him to snap the ball other than when he is ready. This often leads to a poor snap. Therefore, we will put the ball in play whenever the center decides he's ready to snap it.

3. A regulated cadence may be easy for the defensemen to pick up, and if they should get a quick start on their charge because they guessed the snap count, they might be able to block the kick. By snapping the ball silently, the defense loses its quickness.

The signal caller will call the punt in his offensive huddle by simply saying, "Punt with pride—when the center's ready, ready, break!" And punt with pride you must!

FORMATIONS DETERMINE BLOCKING RULES

Many times coaches will be scratching their heads to figure out why they can't seem to get a punt off successfully. One of the reasons might be that the blocking rules in the line do not fit the type of formation being used. The fact of the matter is that if you are using a spread formation, the blocking rules will be different from those used in a tight formation. Furthermore, blocking rules will change the necessity for special positioning of your backfield and secondary blockers. As a first example, consider the popular spread formation diagrammed in 10-1. Note the positioning of the blocking backs in the gaps between the center and two guards.

THE SPREAD PUNT FORMATION

The duties of the ends on almost every punt formation is the same, that is, release quickly and sprint directly to the ball. Their jobs as blockers are limited, often to nothing more than a "brush-by" type of action. In the spread setup, shown in Diagram 10-1, this end play would make the kicker extremely vulnerable to the outside where defensive ends would be rushing in. Also, since the blocking backs are in the gaps between center and guards, the middle is well protected, therefore, the blocking rules can be made in priority form based on these basic constants that have been determined by the formation itself. Thus we reason out the blocking priorities:

1. The outside gap of each blocking lineman is weak due to the absence of the ends, but the middle is strongly guarded by the blocking backs.
2. First, block any defender who aligns head-on.
3. If no one is head-on, block outside gap.
4. If no one is head-on, and no one is in the outside gap, sprint to coverage route as fast as possible.

A view of these two priorities is shown in Diagram 10-2.

The center is required only to make an accurate snap of the ball and not to concern himself with blocking responsibilities until he sees the kicker catch his snap. The coach should be able to teach the center to snap the ball with the kind of technique that permits him to maintain his balance so that he will not be knocked over backwards. Other than that, the center can only be expected to block the man head-on him and then act as a safety man in the coverage pattern. The spread formation is used for the express purpose of getting the offensive linemen down-field quickly on their coverage and at the same time force the defenders to travel a farther distance to get to the kicker. Their spread alignment allows the defense to penetrate after applying nothing more than a brush-by block, but because of the great splits and the great depth of the kicker, the defenders seldom get to the kicker. This type of punt formation demands precise timing between the center and the kicker, and should your center or your kicker be anything short of excellent at their respective duties, this formation should be abandoned. Instead of spreading your line and setting your kicker twelve to fifteen yards deep, we suggest the tight punt formation.

THE TIGHT PUNT FORMATION

The tight punt formation has many more advantages to our way of thinking than does the spread formation. First of all, by virtue of the tight splits taken by the linemen, the efficiency of protection

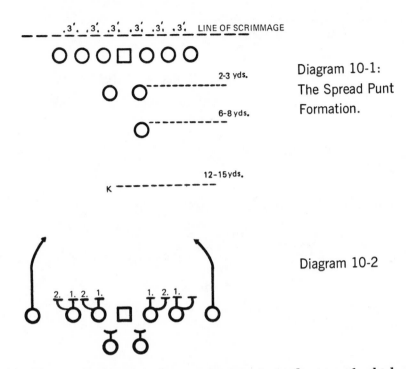

Diagram 10-1:
The Spread Punt
Formation.

Diagram 10-2

afforded the punter is at maximum. Second, since the kicker is no deeper than twelve yards and may even be as shallow as ten yards, the degree of difficulty of snapping the football back is greatly reduced. For high school competition where the accent is on kicking properly and the dangers of an explosive kick return are not so great, the tight punt should be more popular than it is. Third, since high school teams are more likely to gamble with the fake punt, the tight punt formation is more easily adaptable to running plays. The reason for this is because the blocking backs and the linemen are in close proximity to each other and execution of running plays is simple. Diagrams 10-3 and 10-4 represent two of the more popular types of tight punt formations in use today.

The blocking scheme for tight punt formation blocking changes since the ends are protected by the blocking backs. In the double wing setup, the ends release immediately while the two wing backs protect their inside gap. In the T setup, the left halfback will protect against defenders who come in from the left, and the right halfback will protect against penetration from the right. In both setups, the middle area is protected by the third setback. The diagrams show how these assignments are carried out by the blocking backs. (See Diagrams 10-5 and 10-6.)

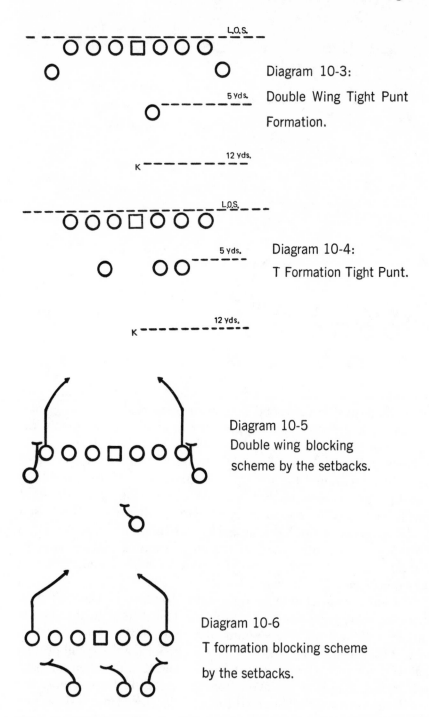

Diagram 10-3:
Double Wing Tight Punt
Formation.

Diagram 10-4:
T Formation Tight Punt.

Diagram 10-5
Double wing blocking
scheme by the setbacks.

Diagram 10-6
T formation blocking scheme
by the setbacks.

This scheme changes the blocking rules for the linemen from what they were in the spread formation. Now, since the blocking backs are responsible for the penetrating defensive ends, the linemen must change their priorities. In the spread formation the linemen concerned themselves with head-on first and outside gap second. In the tight punt formation, however, the second priority becomes inside gap. Thus, the blocking rules in tight punt formation are:

1. Block the defender head-on.
2. If no one is head-on, block the defender in your inside gap.
3. If no one is head-on, and no one is in the inside gap, sprint downfield to your coverage zone.

The comparison of the two different blocking schemes is pictured in Diagrams 10-7 and 10-8.

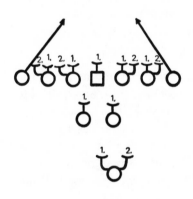

Diagram 10-7

Blocking priorities for the spread punt formation.

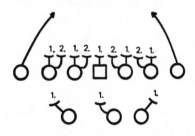

Diagram 10-8

Blocking priorities for the tight punt formation.

A complete acceptance and understanding of these blocking rules is necessary before any discussion of how the block is affected can be brought about. The entire theory of punt protection blocking parallels what we know as area or zone blocking.

AREA BLOCKING

Once the blocker has identified his assignment, he will block him with the same techniques as those advocated in area type pass protection. He will do the following:

1. Keep his head and eyes up, identifying the defender he is to block.
2. Effect his block from a two-point stance that is well-balanced and ready for contact.
3. Step laterally without giving ground to meet the defender squarely, using the chest and fists as points of contact.
4. Maintain contact for at least two seconds before releasing downfield for coverage of the kick.

The main difference between punting and passing as far as the offensive blocker is concerned is that less blocking time is required to make a successful kick. In contrast, a successful drop-back pass requires between five and seven seconds of blocking, whereas a successful punt only requires about two to three seconds of blocking, provided the snap from center is direct and flawless. Since the amount of time is much less for the execution of the kick, the blocker will not give ground or retreat through the course of his punt block. But one point should be understood: the deeper your punter lines up, the less time is required for blocking; the closer to the line he is, the more time is required for blocking. Therefore, there will be a difference in blocking time for the spread and tight punt formations.

THE QUICK KICK

Almost a forgotten weapon in football today is the quick kick. It is a surprise weapon used to get rid of the football when field position is extremely bad. More often than not, the quick kick is used on third down, when the offense is deep in its own territory, (inside its own five yard line), and when the yardage for a first down is more than ten yards. The surprise comes from the fact that the quick kick is executed from the normal offensive formation with no special setup for the kicker. Since the defense may not expect this kick, it will not have a return man back to catch the kick, and the offense may get itself out of the hole.

BLOCKING FOR THE QUICK KICK

The fact that the kicker is probably no deeper than five yards from the line of scrimmage means that the blockers in the line must stop the defensive penetration right at the line of scrimmage. Consequently, coverage on a quick kick is left to the ends. The blockers in the line should use the chop blocking technique as described in the passing game. On the snap of the ball, the blocker will fire-out at the defender's thighs using his shoulder as the surface of contact. The blocking priority for the line would be the same as for the tight punt formation, i.e., head-on first, inside gap second. Once the kick is away the linemen must show their pride by hustling downfield into the coverage pattern. Regardless of the type of formations used, the blocking rules and the chop technique are the best ways to execute the quick kick block.

COVERING THE KICK FROM SCRIMMAGE

This phase of the kick from scrimmage, either a punt or quick kick, involves one common denominator: *pride*, for no matter how good the kicker is, and no matter how well protected he was, the defense will return that kick right back where it came from unless your linemen sprint to their proper positions in the coverage pattern. In order to insure that the linemen get into their coverage routes properly and with maximum quickness, several key techniques must be mastered:

1. While blocking at the line of scrimmage, the lineman must never turn his shoulders. He must remain perfectly square, always facing upfield.

2. After making his block effective, the lineman must get an outside release from the man he is blocking. This outside release allows the blocker to keep from getting tied up at the line of scrimmage and also puts him into the proper route for containing the return man.

3. He must be able to cover a distance of forty yards in less than six seconds if he is to be an effective member of the punting team.

THE FANNING-OUT TECHNIQUE

Once all aspects of the punting game have been fully understood, and the right personnel have been selected for the various skills, the final job for the coach is to outline the actual coverage routes and theory of coverage to stop the dangerous return. What can hurt the kicking team most is loafing. Every member of the offensive unit must sprint to his position in the coverage—this is where *pride* comes in. Second, a great danger to the kicking team is allowing the return man to get to the outside. If this happens, the return man will be able to pick up his blockers, and what was a strategic move by the offense could turn into a touchdown against it. All linemen must insure that the return man is kept inside them. Third, all danger to the offense occurs when players from the kicking team miss their tackles. Consequently, we teach unselfish tackling on kick coverage, which means

The Fanning-Out Technique

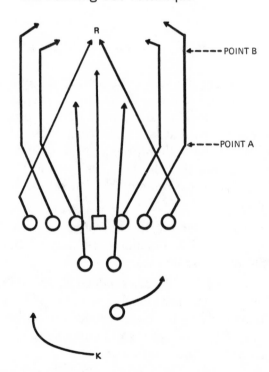

Diagram 10-9: Coverage Routes for All Linemen.

that the entire offensive unit must corner the return man, keeping him inside them, and then gang tackle him. If the ends are able to make the tackle before anyone else gets downfield, that's fine, but generally their job is to cover the kick in case of a fumble and to pressure the return man into running up the middle rather than to the outside. The proper coverage routes for all linemen are pictured in Diagram 10-9.

Of special note is the manner in which the tackles and guards have fanned-out in order to get to the outside of the return man. Once they reach point A, they begin running straight down the field. Throughout their route to the return man, the linemen must make certain that their distance away from each other is always five yards. If they allow themselves to get bunched up, a sudden change of direction by the return man will outmaneuver two or more linemen. Finally, when the linemen get to point B, they get into a break-down position and gradually converge on the ball carrier. This fanning-out technique ensures that the return man will not get to the outside, and that the return man will be gang tackled. To teach it properly, it must be drilled every day for at least fifteen minutes. The drills should be with and without live work, but always with full speed sprinting, and always with *pride*.

chapter 11

How to Block for Kick-Offs

Any time a coach puts players on the field with the specific duty of blocking, he should have prepared them with the finest techniques and methods available to get the job done right. Receiving the opening kick-off is as important an offensive play as the third down situation, or any other crucial situation in football. Why not make it work for a touchdown? Imagine the shock of your opponent if you should break the opening kick-off for a score. The same holds for any time during the game when your teams lines up to receive. There are situations more serious, of course, such as the kick-off that starts the second half when you are losing by only a few points, or the kick-off immediately following your opponent's score in a close contest. Respect for this phase of offensive line play demands that adequate time be spent developing return patterns and skills in blocking for the return men. Pride in our jobs as coaches demands that we hold this play in high regard as a true game breaker, a play that could easily be your best offensive weapon.

ADVANTAGES OF RECEIVING THE KICK-OFF

Did you ever wonder why most coaches have their team captains elect to receive the opening kick-off rather than kick-off to their opponent when they win the coin toss at the beginning of the game? It is most likely that if you were to ask a great many coaches why they like to receive rather than kick-off, you will get answers like, "I consider it good luck to receive first," or "We don't have a very good kick-off man," or "I leave that decision up to the captains, after all it's their team." To our way of thinking these are all invalid reasons. We insist that upon winning the toss of the coin, our captains always elect to receive, and at practice we treat this phase of the game with as much importance as our running game or our passing game. Our reasons for wanting to receive the football are as follows:

1. When the opponent kicks-off, he is obligated to obey the rules that govern the defense, and we are obligated to obey the rules that govern the offense. We always want to be on offense.

2. The kick-off team, unlike any other defensive alignment, has only one line of defense, i.e., the eleven men running hell bent for the return man. There are no linebackers, and no defensive secondary.

3. The eleven men on the kick-off team must protect their zones diligently until the ball carrier begins to run with the ball. Thus, there is little chance for gang tackling. A truly talented return man can elude this one line of defense.

4. More often than not, a coach will put his subvarsity players on the kick-off team, and in their intense desire to impress the coach, they may run without discipline after the ball carrier leaving large holes in the line of chargers.

5. While the defense has only one line of defense, the offense still has the ability to run a variety of plays that can easily outmaneuver the opponent. It is also possible for the receiving team to kick or punt the ball upon receiving it, and this could truly hurt the defense since it is not in a position to return such a kick.

6. The discipline that goes into coaching the receiving of the kick-off far exceeds the amount of training that goes into the training of kick-off coverage. This fact alone has great significance in many close ball games. The receiving team will be better trained for the kick-off than the kicking team will be.

7. You can score when you receive—not when you kick!

THE STANCE

In all my years as a coach I have never seen any team line up to receive the kick-off in any position other than a two-point stance with hands on knees. We also advocate this position, as we do in all phases of the kicking game, and for several reasons:

1. Since the blockers will have to drop-back in order to pick up their blocking assignments, the two-point stance is more conducive to this "retreat."

2. In the event that the kicking team tries to confuse blocking assignments by crisscrossing, the blocker can see clearly the shape the kick-off team is taking as it covers the kick. Visibility is a definite advantage to the two-point stance.

3. Since many of our blocking patterns involve cross-blocking, the two-point stance gives us the advantage of great movement and lateral quickness while retreating to block and form the blocking pattern.

INITIAL STEPS

The initial steps taken by the blocking unit will be different depending on the type of return setup planned, but by and large there is one basic thing that the receiving team must do every time it accepts the kick-off. This "initial step" is taken in retreat as the kicking team approaches the ball. The blockers drop-back slowly keeping their shoulders parallel with the line of scrimmage defined by the forty yard line. During their drop-back, the blockers on the receiving team keep their shoulders square and their eyes glued on the football until after it is kicked. This assures that should the kick be short or the football deliberately kicked onside, the blockers will be alert enough to recover it. Actual contact with the defender does not have to be made until such time as the ball carrier is ready for the blocking pattern to form. For this reason there is no need for the blocker to sprint back to his position, and it is more important that he check for the short kick before getting to his blocking assignment.

THE BLOCKING TECHNIQUE

Kick-off return blocking is identical with man-for-man pass blocking using the same techniques as those described for the drop-back pass. Once the blocker has taken his proper drop-back depth and has picked up his man, he will make contact squarely with the Drive Block Technique. Once contact is made the blocker must rise-up and accelerate and drive the defender completely off the field if possible. Chop blocking, or blocking below the waist is not only an illegal block in the kicking game, but it is also inefficient. Because the kickoff return pattern requires very little blocking time for success, it is possible for a blocker to attack more than one defender. However, the discipline required for the effective blocking on the return demands simply that each blocker take care of one man and do so efficiently. Thus, we combine the techniques of the man-for-man drop-back pass block, and once contact is made, we have the blocker resort to a run-through block and drive the defender out of the play.

TIMING THE KICK AND THE BLOCK

The real key to effective blocking on the kick-off is timing between the receiver's catch of the kick and the execution of the line's block. If the linemen block too soon, they will lose contact with the defender, and he will recover in time to make the stop. This is the greatest single factor of inefficient kick-off return blocking. The procedure for insuring that the timing is perfect is as follows:

1. The depth of the blockers' drop-back is directly proportional to the height and depth of the kick; the higher and deeper the kick, the deeper the linemen drop back. If the kick is low and short, the drop-back is shallow.

2. The linemen must keep their assigned defender in sight at all times as soon as they know that the kick is not onsides. His drop-back will be at the proper depth as determined by the kick, and at the proper angle, as determined by the way his man covers the kick.

3. The blocker should not make contact with the defender until after the kick has been caught. He will know that the reception has been made by a verbal signal given by the receivers waiting for the ball. When one of the receivers has caught the ball, the others around him will yell "Go!"

4. Discipline must be such that at the point of the reception and the verbal signal, "go," every block is executed. Not one block should be executed before this command is given. Coaches may use the analogy of the screen pass as an example of the same type of timing and verbal command.

Without serious drilling, this kind of teamwork and timing can never be achieved. The success or failure of the kick-off should not be left to chance, nor should it be left up to the sub-varsity players. We contend that receiving the kick-off, like every other aspect of this great game, must be handled by your very best players. Unlike the punt or the quick kick, speed in your linemen is not vital, but I suggest that maturity and discipline are. Having been very serious about this phase of offensive blocking, we devote 5 minutes a day practice time to kick-off return blocking.

VARIATIONS IN KICK-OFF RETURNS

In the diagrams that follow, the reader will see some popular kick-off return blocking patterns. In each one, the blocking techniques described are to be used, including stance, initial steps, blocking techniques and timing.

KICK-OFF RETURN MIDDLE

The majority of returns used today can be run from any number of alignments, but the alignment we find most conducive to effective receiving as well as effective blocking, is the 5-3-2-3 setup, and all our returns are based on this setup. (See Diagrams 11-1 through 11-3.)

If the timing is perfect, the number 5 man on the kick-off unit should never get to the ball carrier. Therefore, as shown in Diagrams 11-2 and 11-3, we do not assign any man to block them. This gives us maximum concentration on our blocking at the point of attack.

THE SIDELINE RETURN

Since most kick-off units are manned by sub-varsity players, the tendency is for these players to run directly towards the return man rather than to stay in their respective lanes. Consequently, the kick-

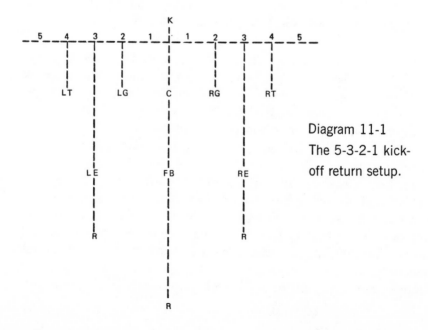

Diagram 11-1
The 5-3-2-1 kick-off return setup.

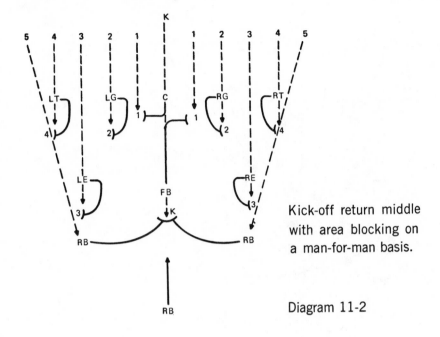

Kick-off return middle
with area blocking on
a man-for-man basis.

Diagram 11-2

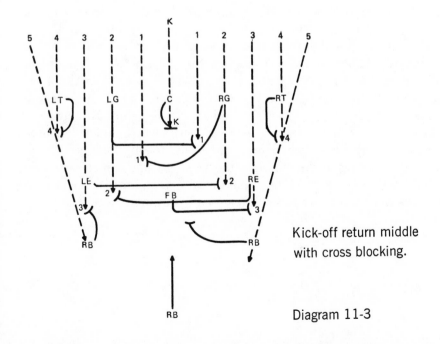

Kick-off return middle
with cross blocking.

Diagram 11-3

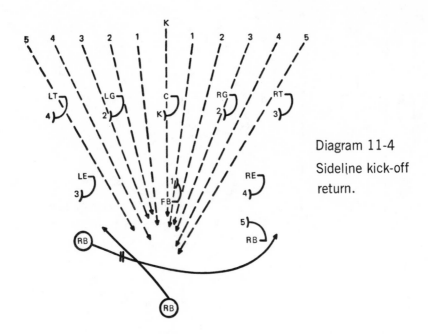

Diagram 11-4
Sideline kick-off
return.

off team will close in on the ball leaving the outside areas vulnerable. Diagram 11-4 represents one kind of sideline return pattern that will take advantage of a team that is guilty of this kind of coverage.

Each blocker in the sideline kick-off return has a specific assignment, the same man-for-man principle as in the middle return. An added attraction is the use of crossing between two return men. This action encourages the defense to converge on an area away from the intended area of the return. It also has the effect of taking one or two defenders out of the play without assigning a man to block them. As you will see, the number one man next to the kicker is left unblocked, while every defender closest to the side of the return is assigned a blocker. This return may be reversed and reverse action between receivers may be switched or even faked, the options are many. Serious coaching in this phase of the kicking game can reward your efforts with a quick touchdown, and maybe even a psychological advantage over the area's favorite team and your arch rival.

chapter 12

Blocking for Extra Points and Field Goals

When the time comes for you to send your extra point or field goal team on to the field, chances are that your offensive blockers have already done a pretty fair job of blocking for the running game or of protecting the passer. Now the time has come for your offense to put the icing on the cake, either with the extra point that will increase your winning margin, or with the field goal that will put the game out of your opponent's reach. Many football games are won or lost here, and even more so today, the extra point and field goal are rated very high in a coach's offensive priority list. It goes without saying then, that the techniques involved in blocking for this phase of offensive football demands serious attention. This chapter alerts the reader to some of the techniques that will insure consistent blocking for extra points and field goals.

STANCE

As in other forms of the kicking game, we strongly advocate the use of the two-point stance in extra points and field goal attempts. The reasons are simple and are based on common sense:

1. The two-point stance allows greater visibility, a vital necessity against defenses who are trying to block place-kicks. The blocker will not see conventional alignments, and the two-

point stance will permit him to recognize the proper blocking assignment with greater ease.

2. Since the blocker is not expected to fire-out and block the defender, there is no need to get down in a three-point or four-point stance. These stances lend themselves only to lower contact position and quicker starts. The two-point stance puts the blocker in a good hitting position ready to take on the defensive charge most effectively for getting the place-kick away.

3. Place-kicks will only be successful if no defender is allowed to penetrate through the offensive line. Therefore, coaches will try to boost the strength of their offensive line by teaching a "wall" technique of blocking. This wall concept requires that a two-point stance be used.

INITIAL STEPS

Unlike the punt formations, on extra points and field goals there is no one assigned to block in the middle area. Both the holder and the kicker are useless as blockers, therefore, we have only nine men who can effectively block the defense. The most vital and most vulnerable area is straight up the middle. The center is primarily involved with the snap pass to the holder, so he too is less than a great asset to the blocking unit. For these reasons, the blocking rules would be given in the following priorities:

1. Block inside gap area first

2. If no one attempts to penetrate the inside gap, then block the man head-on.

For all intents and purposes, every blocker will block towards his inside gap, and only his inside gap; the second priority seldom presents itself. In order to accomplish this blocking task successfully, the entire blocking unit, except the center, must take a lateral jab-step to the inside. This jab-step will draw the blocker's body over into that gap so as to close off any opening that might be there by virtue of a middle attack on the center. *No other steps should be taken,* the outside foot should remain in place, and the blocker will not try to move the defender. The initial step, coupled with the blocker's extended body and his strength of balance is sufficient obstacle to prevent penetration by the defender. This is basically all we mean to do.

TYPE OF BLOCK USED

If we had to name the type of block used in extra point and field goal situations, we would refer to the far shoulder block described in Part I. The far shoulder block in this case, however, is not designed to cut off pursuit or move the defender, but by virtue of the use of the body in the far shoulder technique, we get a very fine block for these types of kicks. The essentials of the far shoulder block that should be stressed in extra point and field goal blocking are the following:

1. The initial step is taken with the near foot into the inside gap.
2. This step forces the blocker's body to be extended across the inside gap preventing penetration.
3. If contact is to be made with a defender, the blocker's head is across the line of charge and the surface of contact will be the outside or far shoulder.
4. The forearms are up high and are held rigidly so that the blocker has a greater blocking surface with which to work.

Any attempt by the blocker to drive or maneuver the defensive man would create an opening between himself and his neighboring lineman. This is a major flaw and would spell disaster for the kicking team.

THE WALL CONCEPT

In order to encourage the blockers to form a wall with their respective far shoulder blocks, we add one small technique to their assignments. When the ball is snapped, the blockers will take their jab-step to the inside and slightly backward. Because we are in a very tight alignment to begin with, this gives the same effect as overlapping, and this coupled with the extension of the body and the use of the far shoulder block help solidify the wall—like appearance of the entire blocking scheme. The following diagram indicates what the total effect looks like on paper. (See Diagram 12-1.)

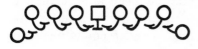

Diagram 12-1

Blocking with the wall concept.

H

K

The coach should emphasize the fact that the wall is a unit blocking technique that can be perfect only when every man does exactly what he is supposed to do each and every time. He should also stress that the head and eyes must always be up, with the neck bulled, and arms high and always prepared for sudden contact.

A WORD ABOUT TIMING

Naturally, all the technique in the world is useless if you have a poor center, a "chicken-legged" kicker, or if the holder can't catch. We must assume that these other aspects of the game are at least satisfactory. The question of timing has always been applied to just these people, i.e., the center's snap, the holder's placement, and finally the kicker's approach and ultimate kick. But the blockers also have a timing responsibility, and I doubt whether or not many coaches are aware of this fact. The timing in the line comes from the speed with which the blockers take their jab-step. If, for example, the left guard steps down to the inside a split second quicker than the left tackle, then we have a problem in timing. Each and every member of the blocking unit must take the initial step simultaneously in order to prevent holes in the wall. When specialty period is being conducted at your practices this fall, see to it that the offensive linemen are perfecting this specialty also, for without this kind of timing, the greatest kicker will never get the ball off successfully.

COVERING THE FIELD GOAL

If all goes well in the line, but the kick for the extra point is missed, there is no chance that the defense can advance the ball. The rules state that in such a case the ball is dead. However, the try for a field goal is a scrimmage kick, and like the punt, a field goal that does not score points can be returned. Also, a blocked field goal can be recovered or advanced. Therefore, even though the blocking techniques are similar, the requirements for alertness are distinctly different. Perhaps the best advice that could be given in order to prevent any laziness in covering field goal attempts by the interior linemen, is to encourage them to cover all kicks, extra points included. This way, habit will dictate that coverage of all kicks is as vital as blocking for the kick. The coverage routes and philosophy outlined for the punting game would be a good guideline for field goals as well.

Again, as in all phases of football, *pride* must be instilled in every player.

CONCLUDING REMARKS

This chapter completes the phases of football that require effective and consistent offensive line play. It has been our intention to provide the reader with techniques that are up-to-date yet fundamentally sound. Furthermore, the material discussed in these chapters has pertained to actual on-the-field work, both at practice and in game conditions. The following chapters are also up-to-date and fundamentally sound, but unlike the techniques of offensive line play, the contents of the next three chapters may be used at any time of the year, in-season or out-of-season. I hope that you will find something of value for your program there.

part V

How to Help
Your Linemen
Prepare Physically

chapter 13

Developing
a Weight-Training Program

Football is a demanding sport. It takes its toll on every player both mentally and physically. As coaches we all recognize the importance of mental preparation, and we take an active part in helping our players develop the right frame of mind for all occasions on the gridiron. The physical preparations are often left up to the individual player, and coaches will either avoid talking about physical preparation because they are unfamiliar with the various techniques, or they stress the need verbally, but without any real push. This is not to say that coaches are not advocates of physical conditioning, they most certainly are. But there are a number of coaches who do not know how to guide their young men in the best way of preparing themselves physically for football. This chapter will serve coaches as a guide to helping their players develop speed, strength, quickness, endurance and flexibility. Moreover, the information stresses the mental attributes derived from weight-training such as self-confidence, self-discipline, dedication and personal sacrifice, all necessary for successful exercising.

WEIGHT-TRAINING vs. WEIGHT-LIFTING

Just as we stress terminology to our players, terminology here is also important. The weight-trainer is any person who uses some form of weight-resistant exercise to train a part or parts of his body for some specific function. A swimmer whose specialty is the butterfly stroke may use a weighted bar and simulate his stroke with resistance greater than that which he faces in the water. By training his specific muscle groups to move in the butterfly stroke fashion with this extra resistance, theoretically he should be able to pull through the lesser resistance of the water with greater ease. This training method thereby increases not only the strength of his muscle groups, but also the ability of his mucles to make these strokes many more times than usual. This then marks an increase in endurance as well. The football player can also be analyzed in this way. If a guard or a tackle trains his legs to move a 220 lb. weighted object forty or fity times, it should later enable him to use these muscles to run faster, or block with more strength and endurance. This would be especially true if the athlete's opponents were less than 220 lbs. and if he only had to execute a block twenty or thirty times. By actual standards, training with weighted objects allows the athlete to go through more of his actual motions than normal and with greater resistance, so that when he gets into competition he has been trained to go beyond what he will actually be facing. This leads to greater strength and endurance.

The weight-lifter also develops strength, but in much greater proportions than the weight-trainer. The objectives of the two are different. Whereas the trainer is more conscious of endurance, the lifter is only concerned with how much weight he can move. The lifter will often commit himself to three or four basic types of lifting exercises and then concentrate on all the muscle groups that enable him to make the lift successfully. Weight-lifters can not avoid weight-training techniques, but because their goals are higher and more concentrated, the lifter will usually work with weights every day. The weight-trainer uses weight-resistant exercises as an aid to preparing himself physically for the athletic activity he participates in, while weight-lifting is of itself the activity the lifter seeks. Finally, there is associated with the word trainer the connotation that a variety of exercises are used, whereas the lifter will concentrate on lifting weight to an overhead position only.

WEIGHT-TRAINING AND THE OFFENSIVE BLOCKER

Our goal is to train effectively for the specific actions that an offensive lineman will go through during the course of a football game. The necessities of offensive blocking are as follows:

1. Leg power for blocking for the running game.

2. Balance for blocking for the passing game.

3. Quickness and agility for pulling and downfield blocking.

4. Flexibility for injury prevention.

These special areas make up the elements of sound offensive line play. Furthermore, when we instruct our athletes in proper weight-training methods, we encourage them to train in only those areas that are pertinent to their positions and the skills they are required to use in the game. Weight-training programs are therefore geared towards specific goals for each athlete in his own individual role as a player. In this way the athlete is preparing himself in the most efficient manner. To this end, a running back may do more speed exercises than a lineman, and defensive linemen may be required to do more strength exercises than backs. In like manner, the offensive lineman will use weight-training methods to improve his performance as a blocker.

SAFETY RULES

It is best to assume that your players are not experienced with the use of weight-resistant exercises in order to minimize minor injuries sustained in the weight-room. The following safety rules should be explained each and every season, before and after regular season workouts:

1. *Never weight-train alone!* The safety of every individual is of primary concern, and partners are a necessity in order for the weighted bar to be lifted or moved into position. The partners or buddies also serve another purpose and that is, one of peer rivalry. As each man takes his turn to try for a new maximum poundage, the other partners will want to do as well and better. The drive for self-improvement will be far greater than if the athlete were to lift by himself.

2. *Never weight-train without warming up!* The complete warm-up routine will be discussed subsequently, but the time allotted for the warm-up should be no less than twenty minutes, and it should include those exercises that are relevant to the types of programs the athletes are involved in. For example, if the trainer is to train muscle groups in his legs, then the warm-up exercises should involve the legs also. The purpose of this warm-up period is to stretch the muscle groups and get circulation concentrated in the vital areas to be used.

3. *Never try to lift a heavy weight without trials!* There are

proper methods of experimentation for which the trainer can determine what his maximum ability is for each different exercise. The methods are time-consuming and require patience on the part of the trainer, especially the beginner. The novice trainer who picks up the first weighted bar he sees is opening himself up to serious injury and wasted time. Several methods of trials will be discussed later in this chapter.

4. *Never hold your breath when weight-training!* When weight-training, the athlete must move the weighted bar in rhythm with normal breathing. As the weight is raised and lowered, the muscle groups contract and extend. Contracted they are tight and shorter than normal, while extended they are being lengthened by the weight of the bar and are relaxed. The proper breathing technique is a coordination of inhaling and exhaling with raising and lowering the weight. The rule is: *Inhale when lowering or relaxing–Exhale when raising the weight or exerting a force*. By following the proper breathing techniques the athlete is able to train with the proper rhythm and speed. If he starts to work too quickly his breathing rhythm will be broken, and it is likely that he will lose control of the weight. Another danger is holding a breath while exerting a force, which is a common fault committed by young athletes. By holding the breath the trainer could cut off oxygen supply to the blood which would result in temporary dizziness and possible fainting.

5. *Never weight-train without dressing properly!* The proper clothing allows for full and complete extension of all parts of the body involved in the exercises. Proper clothing includes the following:

   a. *Sneakers*—So that the athlete will not slip or slide while trying to lift.

   b. *Short-Sleeve Shirt*—So that the elbows and shoulders are free to move through the various exercises without restriction.

   c. *Gym Shorts*—So that the knees and hips are able to move and flex without restriction through the various exercises.

6. *Never wear rubber or plastic sweat suits!* The rubber or plastic suit is designed to produce perspiration. Since there is always a normal amount of perspiration associated with rigorous

weight-training, the rubber or plastic suit causes too much loss of body water and dehydration can result.

DETERMINING THE AMOUNT OF WEIGHT TO USE

Each athlete must determine by a process of trial and error the maximum amount of weight he can use throughout his weight-training program in each different exercise. Once this amount has been determined, the athlete can begin to train and mark his progress in terms of new poundages added as the weeks go by. There are two methods of experimentation in order to determine the proper amount of weight:

1. Calculating various percentages of body weight for specific exercises. As an example, many weight-trainers follow this guide:

    a. 60% of total body weight for military press.

    b. 85% of total body weight for bench press.

    c. 95% of body weight for the squat for dead lift exercises.

2. The athlete may determine what amount of weight is proper for him by experimenting with various amounts of weight for each exercise he wishes to use in his routine. The trainer will estimate an amount at first and then try to use the weight through at least five repetitions. If he can use the weight too easily, then he should record the amount and increase it the next time he performs the exercise. If the amount was so great that he could not move it through five repetitions, then he must decrease the amount the next time he performs the exercise.

SELECTING THE PROPER EXERCISES

Of major importance in the weight-training program for offensive linemen is that each man be motivated and work towards the same end results. It is imperative that the offensive lineman train towards these goals in an effort to improve himself as a blocker in all phases of the game. Taking a good look at the muscle groups that are required in offensive line play, we decided what areas must be concentrated on. The final analysis is the following:

1. Leg strength is necessary for speed and blocking power.

2. The shoulders, chest and arms should be strong for the rigors of contact in close-line play.

3. The neck and back muscles should be strengthened for added power and injury prevention.

The next job is to see what exercises will tax these muscle groups through exercise and then use them in the weight-training program. As far as offensive linemen are concerned, we advocate one basic exercise, the "clean and jerk." The clean and jerk requires the trainer to lift a weighted bar off the ground, pull it up to his chest while in a standing position and then complete the exercise by jerking the weight to an overhead position with arms fully extended. Breaking down the exercise into its various phases, one can readily see how it encompasses all the vital muscle groups we have singled out for offensive line blocking:

1. In raising the weighted bar from the floor, leg and back muscles are called into action, along with the shoulders and upper arms.

2. The act of pulling the weight to an upright position taxes the arms, shoulders, thighs and neck muscles.

3. The jerking phase requires explosive leg power, strong arms and shoulders.

The only other exercise that is required of our offensive linemen is the bench press. We add this exercise to their program for several reasons; first, most young men already know what the bench press is, and they find it to be a good measure of their strength and a good source of competition. You will often hear your athletes talking about how much weight this one and that one can lift in the bench press. Since the athletes themselves consider it valuable, we incorporate it into the program, even if it gives no more than an added "psyche" factor.

As an exercise, the bench press does have significant physical value. It is the best exercise to develop arm and chest strength without elaborate equipment. Furthermore, it is impossible to perform without at least one buddy, and for this reason alone, having it in the program assures that more than one person will be working-out. Proper execution of both these exercises, the clean and jerk, and the bench press, is what truly makes them worthwhile.

PROPER EXECUTION

The proper technique for executing the clean and jerk should be mastered and is as follows:

1. Approach the weighted bar as it rests on the floor. Come close to the bar so that your shins are against the bar. Feet should be slightly wider than shoulder width, palms of the hands towards the lifter, toes pointed outwardly, feet flat on the floor, and head and eyes looking upward at a point on the ceiling. Diagrams 13-1 and 13-2 show the proper approach position front and profile view.

Diagram 13-1:

Approach Position (front view).

Diagram 13-2:

Approach Position (profile view).

2. As the lifter begins to raise the weighted bar from the floor, he inhales slowly. As the weight comes off the floor, the head and eyes remain fixed on the ceiling. This insures that the lifter will keep his back straight and does the bulk of the lifting with his legs and not with his back. The higher the weight comes up, the easier it will be to get the bar on his chest, therefore, the lifter must rise up on his toes as the weight reaches the highest point possible with the strength of the arm and leg muscles. Diagram 13-3 represents this phase of the clean. The weight has been pulled as high as possible with the arms and legs.

3. At this point the lifter must use a quick dropping action in order to get under the weight. Having pulled the weight as high as possible and having raised up on his toes, the lifter

now drops down to a flat-footed position and squats just enough to catch the weight on his chest. The clean is completed when the lifter stands erect with the weight on his chest. The dropping action is a technique that should be practiced with light weights before a heavier weight is attempted. Diagram 13-4 represents the completed phase of the clean.

4. The lifter is now ready to jerk the weight to an overhead position. By flexing the knees slightly, the act of jerking the weight with an upward thrust will help develop the power needed in offensive line play. As he explodes upwards, the lifter trys to throw his chest and arms through the ceiling. The exercise is complete when the weight is held still for a brief moment, the eyes are looking straight ahead, and the arms are locked stiff. The pulling strength required in the clean coupled with the thrusting power required in the jerk, make this exercise truly the all-around football players exercise. Diagram 13-5 represents the complete clean and jerk.

5. To bring the weight down again, the lifter must do everything in reverse. He inhales slowly and brings the weight from the over-head position down to his chest. There is a slight pause here before the lifter then brings the weight to the floor. He must make certain that in returning the weight to the floor he again is looking up at a point on the ceiling so that he does not inadvertently bend over at the waist and put undue pressure on his lower back.

The bench press technique should also be pointed out to your athletes. The correct execution of this exercise is as follows:

1. The lifter lays flat on his back on a bench that allows his feet to reach the floor and is no more than twelve inches wide so that the lifter's shoulder blades may operate freely. One or two helpers should then lift the weight over the lifter's head and chest at approximately arm's length. See Diagram 13-6.

2. From this starting position the lifter brings the weight down to his chest, inhaling slowly as he does so. The bar should touch the chest but not come down so fast that it bounces back up. See Diagram 13-7.

3. Getting the weight back to the starting position is the completed bench press exercise. Explosiveness and power can be developed along with strength if the lifter will arch his back

Diagram 13-3: The Clean (Phase I).

Techniques:
1. Lifter is inhaling as he lifts.
2. Head and eyes are fixed on ceiling.
3. Lifter is raising up on his toes.

Diagram 13-4: The Completed
Clean (Phase II).

Diagram 13-5: The Clean and Jerk.

Diagram 13-6: Bench Press
(starting position).

Techniques:
1. Back flat on the bench.
2. Feet are flat on the floor.
3. Weight begins at highest
   point with arms fully
   extended.

Diagram 13-7: Bench Press.

Techniques:

1. The lifter is inhaling as he brings the weight to his chest.
2. Back remains flat on the bench.
3. Feet remain flat on the floor.
4. The bar does not bounce off the lifter's chest.

and exhale when pushing the bar back to the over-head position.

The bench press is a good measure of chest and arm strength, and a lift of 300 lbs. or more carries a great deal of respect for the lifter. For incentive, try starting a "300 club" and see how many linemen can make it. As your program gets into full strike, I'm certain that this club will advance to the 400 level.

HOW TO WARM UP PROPERLY

As mentioned earlier, before any exercises are performed with weight-resistant equipment, there should be a vigorous warm-up period of at least twenty minutes. The warm-up is designed to stimulate general body circulation and also stretch the primary muscle groups to be used. The following exercise routine will serve the purpose of warming-up:

Exercise	Repetitions
Jumping Jack	20
Trunk Twister	10 left, 10 right
Neck Bridges	forward and reverse
Groin Stretch	left and right
Toe Touch for Hamstring	20
Push-Ups	20
Sit-Ups	30
Variety of Stretching Exercises	
Clean and Jerk	With very light weights—20 reps.

Each individual trainer should have at this point in his athletic career, a special selection of limbering-up exercises that he uses. These exercises may be substituted for those listed above. In addition, there are many athletes who will find the above exercises insufficient for them. It will be necessary for these people to increase the warm-up period and add certain exercises to this routine.

HOW TO PUT IT ALL TOGETHER

Every player must be willing to sacrifice three days per week for his weight-training program. The three-days per week schedule has been established by a great many coaches and trainers because it allows for the necessary one day's rest between workouts. This day of rest is vital in order for the body cells to rebuild themselves with the nutritional diet that the athlete must follow. It is this constant tearing down and rebuilding of muscle tissue that makes weight-training and nutritional guidance the mainstays of strength building. The resulting growth appears in muscle size, overall body strength, and endurance. Of the possible schedules that will allow the athlete to rest at least one day in between workouts, one alternative is for weight-training on Monday, Wednesday, and Friday, with rest days on Tuesday, Thursday, and the weekend. This day-by-day schedule must be set up in a progressive way. The first day of the work-out week should not be as vigorous as the last day. Each day in the schedule should gradually build up to the last day when the heaviest weights are used. On this last day each trainer should try to use his maximum amounts in each exercise. Doing this at the end of every week, with significant increases in the maximum poundage, is how one will determine his improvement. In order to clarify how the days of the week are to be used, we identify them with special nicknames.

DAY-BY-DAY

The first day of the workout week is called the "tinkering" day, a day when the trainer goes to the weight room and goes through a variety of exercises with light weights and many repetitions. In many respects, the tinkering day is nothing more than a day of limbering up for the harder days yet to come, but more than this, it gives the athlete an opportunity to realize that he has gotten stronger and that his poundages from the week before may have increased. This tinkering prepares him for the second day, which is referred to as a "regular" day. Here the athlete works with his basic exercises for whatever goals he wishes to strive. In the case of offensive linemen, the exercises are merely the clean and jerk, and the bench press. Having warmed up properly, the athlete will go through a minimum of three sets of each exercise, performing a minimum of five repetitions and a maximum of twelve. If the athlete uses the weight room incorrectly, he will gain nothing and lose a great deal of time. Furthermore, results will not be noticed and many young men will lose interest and stop training all together. If the repetitions exceed twelve, then the weight should be increased, and likewise, if the repetitions are less than five, the weighted bar should be lowered. Each week the athlete should increase his poundages and his sets, *never the repetitions!* The number of repetitions will be decreased only on the third and final day of the workout week, the "max" day.

On the third day, the trainer will again warm up properly, and then begin his maximum lifts. His attempts are made in the exact same exercises that he has planned for his individual program; in the case of the offensive linemen, their "max" attempts will be in the clean and jerk, and the bench press. The trainer may go through several sets of warming-up exercises before he attempts his "max," but he should be careful not to tire himself. A "max" lift may simply be defined as that amount of weight in a given exercise which the trainer can move through one complete repetition. Our goals are to be able to record a higher "max" at the end of each week by an average gain of five lbs. per exercise. The following program is recommended for a weekly workout program:

Mon.	Tues.	Wed.	Thur.	Fri.	Weekend
"Tinker" 8 reps. 3 sets 60% of max.	rest	"regular" 5-8 reps. 4 sets 80% of max.	rest	"Max" 1-3 reps. 1-3 sets "MAX"	rest

In the actual workout week this is all the weight-training that is required; however, the days where rest is indicated means that no weight-training is going on, but that other activity is. In the subsequent chapters we will discuss some types of activities that can be used to fill in these rest days.

chapter 14

How to Develop Speed and Quickness

Although many people contend that speed and quickness are mental disciplines, coaches have proven that both can be developed and improved. Coaching experience has provided sufficient evidence that an increase in leg strength and flexibility can help the athlete realize greater overall quickness and an increase in speed over longer distances, especially in the forty yard dash. Speed and quickness are extremely vital to all football players, but more so to the offensive lineman than any other player. In the battle in the "trenches," coaches frequently find that their offensive linemen are out-weighed and often overpowered by bigger and stronger defenders. Speed and quickness are two attributes that not only can nullify the defense's weight advantage, but they can also turn the advantage over to the blocker.

THE ARIZONA STATE PROGRAM

A speed workout program especially for the development of leg strength, leg flexibility, efficient running form, and increased leg stride, all vital to overall speed, was proposed by Arizona State University and is presented here for the benefit of those coaches who have not heard of it or had it explained to them. The program is divided into two parts, and it can be performed on those days in the week when the athlete is not weight-training.

PART I

1. Start on a football field wearing football shoes and begin high knee running, or "knee pumps" at top speed. The knees should be brought up as high as possible with enough gradual forward movement to allow a total of 12 knee pumps for five yards or between 100 and 120 knee pumps for fifty yards. After you have run fifty yards, stop and walk back to starting point.

2. Repeat this technique over a distance of fifty yards again and do so three times. The time between each successive run should not exceed two minutes. The entire workout should not take more than ten minutes.

3. Once the fifty yard distance has been mastered, increase the distance to seventy-five yards.

PART II

1. After a rest of fifteen minutes, move to a track or surfaced field. Start out running with high knee action and very small strides. Gradually increase your strides as you run the length of 100 yards, by which point you should be at maximum stride length. To insure that the stride length is maximum, force yourself to point your toes and actually kick those legs out in front of you.

2. As you begin to run the 100 yard distance, your head and upper body will be bent slightly over your knees. When you lengthen your strides your body should begin to straighten up allowing your legs and knees to lead your body down the field. In order to get the feel for this action, you should try "bounding" down the field in the same manner as a drum major, leaning back as far as you can with your eyes focused on the sky.

3. A combination of high knee action and increased length of stride over a period of time will result in an increase of leg strength, leg flexibility, efficient running form, and overall speed.

Football drills are used with the primary purpose of developing a natural response within the athlete that allows him to execute the desired skills effectively and efficiently every time without the necessity for overconcentration. Blocking, tackling, reading keys, etc., are drilled constantly so that they will become second nature in response to the actual game condition. Since running ability is as vital to football as any of the above mentioned skills, it naturally follows that this skill should also be drilled. Perhaps the greatest single factor in improving speed is in improving running form, for most of what we lack in speed can be traced to wasted body motion through improper running form. The following set of exercises should be incorporated in the speed workout and should be performed prior to actual sprint drills or any other form of speed conditioning:

FORM RUNNING TECHNIQUES AND COACHING POINTS

1. The athlete must relax and get his body into a supple attitude.

2. Always run on the balls of the feet, *never flat-footed!*

3. The toes should always be pointed straight down the field. You will lose distance on every step if the toes are not pointed directly in front of you.

4. Always run in a straight line, for this is the shortest distance to a TD. In timed events, this is vital to a fraction of a second, especially in the forty yard dash.

5. Use the Arizona State Program to determine the proper stride for your height. Overstriding can be worse than understriding.

6. The angle of your body while running is important. You should be leaning forward slightly, head up, hips, shoulders, ankles, and head all in a straight line. Do not run too far bent over or too straight up.

7. Arm action is also important. The opposite arm and leg should move in unison. Keep your arms in against your body. When the arms pump away from the body, excess energy is wasted and there is entirely too much lateral body motion. This is a major error in the form running of every football player.

A SPEED WORKOUT

Running is in itself a form of weight lifting, and the ability to run fast is representative of one's leg power. We have already discussed this point, but the fact remains that if you train by running, eventually you will build up leg strength and power, just as you would if you were to train your arms in the bench press. Therefore, once the athlete has mastered the form running techniques and has found the correct stride length for himself, he can begin to further increase his speed by actually training at it. This training is done through a series of sprints that enable the athlete to increase his speed and endurance at the same time. The procedure is as follows:

1. Begin with ten twenty-yard sprints at 1/2 speed, checking form and stride length.
2. Run ten thirty-yard sprints at 3/4 speed. After each one, walk back to the starting point.
3. Proceed to increase the distance of each sprint five yards every two workout days until you are running forty yard dashes.
4. On the next workout day begin running every other sprint at full speed, and the others still at 3/4 speed.
5. On the third workout day, run every sprint at full speed.
6. On the fourth day, jog back to your starting point instead of walking.
7. Do not add any distance to your sprints and do not try to run more than ten. Instead, try to decrease the amount of time that it takes to run through the entire workout.

Since this is a progressive type of running program, it would best be used in the off-season and, ideally, just prior to the start of a new season. By the time the season starts, not only will the athlete have increased his speed, but he will also be in excellent condition. If the workout is performed with the dedication it requires, the athlete will in effect be sprinting forty yards a total of twenty times with little or no rest in between sprints.

DRILLING FOR QUICKNESS

Quickness is a part of body movement concerned with one's ability to respond immediately to a cue. Like many other skills in football, quickness can be improved and developed through systematic use of drills. The purpose of this section is to discribe some of the better drills used for the purpose of increasing the quickness of the offensive lineman.

Basic philosophy for all quickness drills:

1. The drill should last only for six to twelve seconds, otherwise it becomes an endurance drill.
2. Quickness must be encouraged throughout each drill, and in moving from one drill to another, and in moving from one area of the field to another.
3. The ready position before the drill and the finished position after the drill should be a proper hitting position.

Drill #1: Foot-Fire Drill.

Purpose: To teach offensive linemen to keep their feet moving at all times, regardless of the direction they must turn or the reactions they must make.

Procedure: A group of linemen set up in several rows and columns facing the coach. The first row goes through the drill first, then the second, and the third, etc. On the coach's signal, the players will begin a rapid, piston-like movement of the feet making certain that their weight is balanced on the balls of their feet and that they are maintaining a sound hitting position. Their feet must move quickly and without coming very high off the ground. This action of the feet is the actual "foot-fire."

Variation: After a few seconds of foot-firing, the coach dismisses the first group with a command, and they are to sprint past a designated point. When each group has completed the first exercise, the coach may add some reactions to the actual foot-fire. A common variation is to command the athlete to turn ninety degrees to the right or left with a simple command such as "right" or "left," making certain that the athlete continues to move his feet rapidly even though he has to change his direction.

Drill #2: Mirror Drill.

Purpose: To encourage quickness through a series of maneuvers and through competition. The variations in movement are determined by the participants.

Procedure: Two players, "A" and "B," start by facing each other. "A" will be the designated leader. The two players are separated from each other by ten yards. "A" tries to lose "B" by moving laterally, spinning, rolling, jumping, etc., in an effort to "out-quick" his partner. The second phase of this drill simply makes "B" the leader and he attempts to "out-quick" the other man.

Drill #3: Ups and Downs

Purpose: To help the athlete develop natural quick-footedness, and to encourage him to get up quickly once he has been knocked down on the ground.

Procedure: Have your entire group spread themselves evenly so that they are about five yards apart from each other in all directions. On the coach's signal, all begin to foot-fire in place. From this point until the drill is concluded, all players will continue to foot-fire. The next command by the coach will be "hit it," upon which every player will hit the ground on his belly and get up instantly to his foot-fire position. There is no command to get back up, so the next command will again be "hit it."

Variation: The up-and-down action can be added to almost any quickness drill as the end part of that drill. Once the coach wants to end a drill, he may say, "Hit it," which tells the athlete to hit the ground and sprint to a designated point up field.

Drill #4: Forty Yard Up-and-Back Drill

Purpose: To develop quickness and balance in change of direction. Encourages linemen to be low in order to insure quickness. Also an excellent conditioning drill.

Procedure: The athlete assumes his football stance. On the coach's command he will sprint to a point ten yards away. When he reaches that point, he must touch the ground with both hands, pivot and sprint back to his starting position. When he returns to the starting position, he again pivots in the same manner and then sprints back to another point, only this time it is twenty yards away. The athlete continues to return to the original starting position, but each time he sprints back up field, he sprints an extra ten yards until he reaches a total

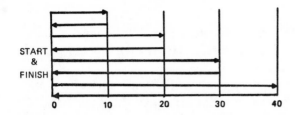

Diagram 14-1:

Up-and-Back Drill.

of forty yards: Diagram 14-1 depicts the actual path of the athlete running this complete circuit.

Variation: As an encouragement to the competitiveness of the athlete, the coach may set several lines of players up against each other to run this drill in a relay race fashion. Also an excellent conditioning drill.

Drill #5: The Box Drill

Purpose: To develop quickness in all directions through various types of footwork.

Procedure: Place four markers in a square as shown in Diagram 14-2. The box should be no smaller than ten yards on each side. From a designated starting point, the athletes run outside the perimeter of the square performing a different running technique along each of the four sides of the square. As he reaches the next corner, and without stopping, the athlete changes his footwork and begins the next technique. A combination of four different running styles may be used as indicated by the diagram (See Diagram 14-2.)

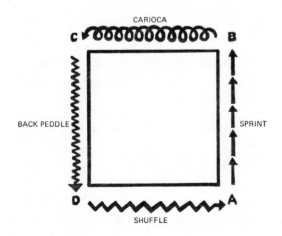

Diagram 14-2:
The Box Drill

Drill #6: Zig-Zag Drill

Purpose: To provide coach and athlete with a change of pace from other quickness drills. Helps develop peripheral vision and balance.

Procedure: Place seven markers about five yards apart from one another and five yards to the left and right of one another in staggered fashion. The athletes start at one end and run through the set up in a forward direction one way, and on the return trip they will run backwards. The cuts made around each marker must be made sharply and not rounded off, otherwise the quickness effect will be lost. (See Diagram 14-3.)

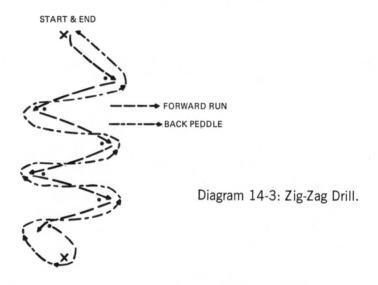

START & END

FORWARD RUN

BACK PEDDLE

Diagram 14-3: Zig-Zag Drill.

Drill #7: Four-Point Explosion Drill

Purpose: To teach offensive linemen to explode into their opponents quickly and to recoil ready to strike again. Develops unity and timing in the line.

Procedure: Use either the two- or seven-man sled for this drill. Have the linemen position themselves as close as possible to the pads of the sled in a four-point stance, i.e., with both hands and both feet on the ground. On the coach's command, all linemen must strike the sled with one explosive burst. All blockers use the same shoulder, and no driving of the machine is permitted. Without any signal from the coach, the players recoil to their four-point stance ready to explode again at the coach's command. Each time the linemen strike, they use the alternate shoulder, and they must never allow their knees to touch the ground. The faster the coach is able to give the commands, the quicker the linemen are becoming. This is also an excellent conditioning drill.

Variation: This drill may also be executed from a six-point position, i.e., both hands, both knees, and both toes touching the ground. As an addition to the repeated striking of the machine by the linemen, the coach may end the drill by having the blockers actually drive the sled for several counts after five or more quick hits.

Drill #8: Skipping Rope

Purpose: To develop leg strength and quick coordination between hands and feet. Excellent for pre-season training.

Procedure: Have the linemen jump for two solid minutes daily. The true test of quickness is total number of successive jumps in the two minute period. Once the athlete can jump the full two minutes without a miss, change the style of footwork being used.

Variations: Normal jumping technique; alternating leg technique; turning rope in reverse; sprint jumping on every turn instead of every other turn of the rope.

Drill #9: Attack Drill

Purpose: To develop overall team quickness in the offensive line and unity in the charge.

Procedure: Best used on the seven-man sled since all the linemen will be involved. Have the linemen position themselves an exaggerated distance off the machine, about three yards, farther than they would normally be from a defender. This excessive distance forces the line to fire-out all the more quickly, since one slow man could cause the entire sled to move erratically. The coach will designate which shoulder is to be used, and on the normal offensive cadence, the linemen will fire-out and block aggressively. Eventually this drill will produce linemen who are completely together as they charge, and the seven man offensive line will meet the defensive front line at the same time. This is the greatest asset of an offensive line.

Variation: The coach may also include play-calling in this drill so that the linemen get accustomed to their quarterback's voice and rhythm. Having several linemen pull out of the line and allow the remaining linemen to attack the sled also helps develop quickness and timing in such plays as powers, sweeps, and traps, and other intricate plays that require extra time in developing execution.

There may very well be a great deal of truth in the belief that speed and quickness are strictly mental attitudes, but rather than leave the development of these vital skills up to chance or mental preparation, we have offered some proven drills that will improve the overall speed and quickness of the entire team, especially the offensive line, where they may be the great equalizers of strength and size.

chapter 15

Helping to Prevent Injuries

Injuries sustained by football players are the result of many things, not all of which can be directly connected with a lack of physical conditioning. Our contention is that many of the injuries that do occur can be prevented ahead of time if some basic exercises are incorporated in the daily practice schedule. If one thinks carefully about the many different ways an athlete may be involved in contact in football, and the many different movements that his body must go through during the course of live practices and games, it should become obvious that injury prevention ranks very high on the list of things to be done in pre-season and during the season. This is a responsibility that must be shared by both coach and athlete.

THE VITAL AREAS

THE NECK

The vital areas of the body are those that are the weakest and, therefore, more susceptible to injury. Starting from the top of the body, the neck is of primary importance. Neck muscles are used in blocking and tackling, and since the head leads the body in motion during contact, it is likely to be hit or met with contact at unexpected moments. These unexpected moments are when most injuries occur, serious as well as minor injuries. Neck injuries can range anywhere from simple soreness to serious damage to the spinal cord.

THE SHOULDER

The next area of concern is the shoulder, a part of the body used also in blocking and tackling, and an area where most athletes sustain an injury at one time or another in their careers. Much of what should be done to strengthen the shoulder would be in the form of simple calisthenics such as pull-ups and push-ups. An injury to the shoulder can also be very serious, though not nearly as serious as a neck injury. One big advantage is that pads are worn to protect the athlete from the contact that this part of the body endures constantly.

THE HIP JOINT

Moving on to the lower part of the body, we find a substantial amount of injuries lately occuring at the hip joint. This injury is especially common to running backs, who may injure themselves trying to pull away from a tackler or who may take a shot to the side from a die-hard tackler. The hip padding worn by most athletes will only prevent hip bruises or "pointers," and even then many players still come up with minor hip injuries. These minor bruises can not always be prevented, but the major ones can. Like the shoulder, the hip exercises would be restricted to simple stretching and flexion movements.

THE KNEE

The fourth area of concern, and the all-time eliminator of football players, is the knee. The knee, like any other joint in the body, is nothing more than a mass of cartilage, tendon, ligament, skin and bone. It is the weakest joint in the human body, and yet it must take the worst beating. Injury to the knee can occur in many different ways, but the most common in football is when the knee sustains contact from the side, either on the inside or on the outside of the joint.

THE ANKLE

The final area that is vital is the ankle. Although not often a serious injury, the loss of mobility by way of an ankle injury can have the same effects as a more serious injury, and that is, the loss of a good ball player. Ankle injuries occur for several reasons, most importantly, because there is no kind of protective gear offered that will protect this part of the body. The resultant injuries can range from a simple sprain to a compound fracture.

Having introduced these vital areas, it is essential now that we discuss ways to prevent injuries to these areas. It must be understood, however, that there is never a guarantee associated with any of these exercises, only satisfaction in the knowledge that we are giving our athletes the best possible coaching in every area of the game, including injury prevention.

THE PROPER EXERCISES FOR THE VITAL AREAS

THE NECK

An excellent exercise for building neck strength is the rigid-body, isometric exercise that involves two athletes and develops neck strength in four areas.

Two players pair off and one will perform the exercise while the other acts as his helper. The exerciser makes his entire body rigid, especially his neck, while his partner places his hands on the exerciser's forehead. Gradually the helper lets the exerciser down slowly towards the ground to an angle of about forty-five degrees. The helper holds his partner there for a count of five seconds and then returns him to the upright position. The helper then goes around to his partner's back, places his hands on the exerciser's helmet, and slowly lowers him backwards to an angle of forty-five degrees with the ground, delays for five seconds, and again returns him to the upright position. These two phases will strengthen the front and back parts of the neck respectively. The third and fourth phases are done in the same manner, only now the helper will let the exerciser be lowered to the ground sideways, first to the right side, then to the left side, always with the five second pause at the forty-five degree angle position. The players will then switch, and the helper will become the exerciser, and vice versa.

Other more common exercises, such as the wrestler's bridge and weight resistant exercises, are also very good out-of-season, but the rigid-body exercise described above will fit very well into the regular season on a daily basis because it only takes a few minutes for a great many players to perform, and it is extremely thorough for all the muscles of the neck.

THE SHOULDER

Coaches should advocate shoulder exercises of all kinds, not so much because shoulder injuries are serious, but because these injuries tend to depress the athlete and discourage him from playing. In truth, there are more minor shoulder injuries than there are serious ones, but the young athlete uses his shoulder in so many skills that, should he sustain an injury to this area, he will instinctively shy away from contact even though the injury is not all that serious. Therefore, as well as being physically beneficial, these exercises give the athlete a psychological boost in that after he has completed certain exercises, he will be more confident that he has a good, strong pair of shoulders. In the area of physical conditioning and strength building, if the athletes truly believe that they are stronger and better able to meet the demands of the collisions in football, chances are they will hit harder, be more aggressive, and sustain fewer injuries in the long run.

Two very excellent shoulder exercises that can be done daily are the rope climb and the pull-up. The deterrent to these two exercises may be the lack of proper equipment. However, time permitting the athletes may climb the rope in the gym and use the pull-up bar indoors prior to coming out on the field. These two exercises can also be done with full practice gear on, adding a resistance effect to the exercise. If an indoor facility is not available, then perhaps some of the players could organize a group of volunteers to help construct a chinning bar right out on the practice field. Athletes who are dedicated enough to build up their own facilities will certainly continue their dedicated attitude in preparing themselves physically for the rigors of football.

THE HIP

Without a doubt, the hip joint is the most neglected part of the anatomy when it comes to exercising. Yet, recent studies have shown that a more supple, flexible hip joint can be the greatest differential in the increase of speed. The exercises require very little time and, again, should be done daily. Two excellent exercises are described below.

First, both exercises require two partners, one who will actually perform the exercise, and one who will act as a helper. To begin, the exerciser places his hands on his partner's shoulders and stands erect facing him. Keeping one foot planted on the ground, he will swing the other leg across his body and out to the side five times. He does this with a rigid leg so that the strain is on the hip joint. He then repeats the exercise with his other leg. As he rests, his helper will do the same routine with both legs. The first man begins again, only this time he increases the number of "kicks" and tries to kick even higher than the first time. When each man has gone twice, the exercise is complete.

The second hip loosening exercise is one that resembles running in place. Again, two players will pair off facing one another, the exerciser with his hands on his helper's shoulders. On a command by the coach, the exerciser will run at a very slow pace overemphasizing high knee action. His helper can even put his hands up as a high target for the exerciser's knees to hit. The first phase of this exercise should be a count of ten to fifteen steps. The players then switch and the helper goes through the same exercise. For the second phase the number of steps increases, the speed increases and the height of the knee action must be kept the same. In this way we get great flexion of the hip while at the same time encouraging quickness and speed. Once both players have gone through this routine, the coach may end the drill by having them stride two twenty-yard sprints at 3/4 speed emphasizing high knee action in the same manner as a drum major marching down the field.

THE KNEE

Knee injuries occur most frequently when the athlete is hit when he least expects it. Unfortunately, many knee injuries are also the result of illegal blocking, and apart from coaching players in ways to strengthen themselves for the sake of injury prevention, coaches should also preach fair play in all phases of the game so that no player is injured unnecessarily. Legal blocking and preventive exercises are two major ways to avoid the dreaded knee injury. Another remedy that coaches may find of value is in a change of shoes. The standard football shoe, with the regulation cleats, provides the athlete with a great traction, but to a certain extent it also prohibits a great deal of the flexibility needed to sustain the impact of collision. Consider the running back who gets hit from the side and is spun around by the contact of two or more tacklers. If the ball carrier's body and legs are twisted, it follows that his feet must also twist on the ground. But since the football cleats are dug deep into the ground, the pivoting of the knee, ankle and feet is extremely cut down. Therefore, the brunt of the twisting action is sustained by the knee and the ankle and the result is very often a serious injury. In order to cut down on this type of injury, we insist that all of our ball players wear a shoe with a molded sole at practice as well as in ball games. Many companies are now selling a molded sole type football shoe for use on artificial surfaces, and these types of shoes are excellent, but the standard soccer shoe is also excellent and may even be more desirable since it is a lighter weighted shoe. Our players have found that not only do they suffer less strain on their knees, but also, the molded sole shoe will not pick up the mud and grass clods on a wet field the way regular football shoes do. Consequently, the athlete feels lighter afoot in all kinds of field conditions, which we consider a major psychological advantage.

Once these ideas are put into the program, the exercises will further reduce the chances for an injury. One very good knee exercise is one where the athlete takes his knee in hand and actually works on loosening it up. The athlete will lie on his back holding one leg off the ground with both hands under his thigh. He then begins to rotate the uplifted knee in circular motions, first in circles to the right and then in circles to the left. Having completed ten circular motions with one knee, he begins the other knee up and goes through the same routine. He will go through this process with each knee as much as three times, increasing the number of circular motions each time, until he feels that he has loosened the knee up sufficiently.

There are other exercises that may be beneficial for the knee also, but of utmost importance is that no exercise be done with "bouncing." The "squat" exercise has always been considered a valuable form of knee flexion, yet it has come under heavy criticism by those who feel that the squatting movement does more harm than good. The argument against this opinion is simply that when squats are executed by athletes, they must be done slowly and without bouncing. If the athlete attempts to do a full squat movement prior to proper warm-up, then damage to the knee is possible. But those who are familiar with the exercise know that this is the case with all exercises, not just the squat. We are confident that the squat can be an effective knee exercise if the athlete will warm up properly, exercise slowly, and avoid bouncing throughout the movement.

THE ANKLE

The injuries sustained by the ankle are seldom as serious as those sustained by the neck, shoulder, or knee, but even a minor injury to the ankle can rob the athlete of the kind of mobility required to play at full speed and avoid other more serious injuries that could be a result of favoring a minor bruise or twist. Players who insist on participating with minor injuries are often susceptible to more serious injuries for the simple reason that their minor injury prevents them from hustling or moving quickly enough to avoid getting hurt. There are many things that the athlete can do in order to reduce the chances of an ankle injury, one of which is the use of a low-cut style football shoe with the molded sole. A shoe of this type allows maximum freedom and flexibility so that when the ankle is hit or twisted in a strange manner, it will yield to the stress and survive without injury. The athlete may also wear simple ankle wraps or elastic bandages for extra support. In cases where weak ankles are the athletes problem, daily taping should not be neglected, especially when heavy contact drills are going to be conducted. Once these preventive actions are followed, there are several exercises that can be employed by the athlete and the coach to assure that every precaution has been taken.

To stretch the ankle, sit on the floor and bend the left knee so that it can be comfortably reached. Grab the ball of the foot with the left hand and the ankle with the right hand. Then manipulate the foot in a full circle stretching the ankle in all directions. Finish stretching the left ankle by extending the left knee while holding the ball of the left foot and steadily pulling back towards you. The second phase of the exercise is to change ankles and repeat the process.

A second exercise for the ankle is to actually walk up the side of a hill sideways so that the right foot is above the left, then walk down the hill the same way, and finally change directions so that the left foot is above the right. The extension accomplished by this exercise can also be done by walking on the outside of the ankle with knees wide apart, and then walking on the inside of the ankle with knees together.

Although these areas are what we consider the vital areas of concern, there are other parts of the anatomy that require attention. These are the more common areas of concern, areas that are generally exercised daily. However, so that no stone is left unturned, we offer the reader a special technique for properly stretching these areas of the body that may also sustain uncomfortable and annoying injuries.

COMMON PREVENTIVE EXERCISES

Aside from the usual exercises that are performed almost universally at every practice session, there is a routine that we have our players go through daily that we feel has been a major reason why few of our players have sustained serious injury. We consider these exercises as preventive in nature but, at the same time, they are designed to flex the more common areas of the body. The main point in this section is a technique that requires that the athlete pull through the stretching action as opposed to the more popular way of "bounding" practiced by most athletes. The pull technique is similar to the procedure in isometric exercises where the athlete gradually increases the amount of effort he puts into the pull for a duration of five counts. Using this technique, we find that the athlete is better prepared and equipped with the flexibility and looseness required to sustain collisions in football games and live practice drills. The technique applied to several exercises appears below.

The Hamstring Exercise
1. Stand with both feet close together; bend at the waist keeping knees rigid; on coach's command to pull, reach down and grab your ankles as you try to pull your helmet to your knees. Apply steady pressure for a count of five seconds, constantly trying to get your helmet to your knee and keeping those knees rigid. One time only.
2. Cross the right leg over the left leg in a standing position. Keep the back knee rigid and on the command to pull, again try to get the helmet to the knee while grasping the ankles. Hold this steady pulling action for a count of five. Do this one time only, then switch leg positions.

The Hurdler's Stretching Exercise
1. Sit down on the ground; pull your right ankle behind you and hold it close to the side of your butt with your right hand; keep your left leg flat on the ground; make certain that the split between your legs is as wide as you can make it; keep your left leg completely rigid; grasp your left ankle with your left hand and on the coach's command to pull, touch your helmet to your left knee; pull at a steadily increasing rate so that the hamstring of your left leg begins to burn; never bounce and never allow your knee to bend.
2. Remain in this position; now lay back keeping the right leg bent and close to your butt while the left leg is still rigid and flat on the ground; the pulling action now is performed with the knee of the right leg; on coach's command to pull, force your right knee down to the ground at a steady pulling rate; keep your left knee rigid and do not bounce. The area across the top of the thigh will be getting stretched in this phase of

the exercise, an area where very sore pulls are often a problem.

3. Having completed one set of each of these exercises, tuck the left leg close to your butt and extend the right leg simply reversing the position. Go through the same routine again.

Stretching the Groin

1. Stand facing the coach with your legs as far apart as you can get them and still be comfortable; bend the right knee and turn towards it so that your chest is directly on top of the right knee; keeping your left leg rigid, when the coach says pull, pull and stretch your whole body towards that bent knee; again maintain a steady pull for five seconds, then relax. Next, turn to your left and bend the left knee and go through the same routine.

2. Remain in this spread position; bend at the waist keeping both knees rigid. On coach's command to pull, the athlete pulls down as far as he can forcing both his hands and his helmet in between his legs. He does not bounce nor does he relax, but he must maintain a steady pulling motion between his legs for a five second count. This exercise is also done only one time for the five counts.

Complete Leg and Groin Exercise

1. Players should pair off so that one performs the exercise while the other acts as a helper. The helper bends over at the waist with his elbows on his knees so that his back is flat and parallel with the ground. The exerciser puts his right leg up on the helper's back and makes certain that both knees are kept rigid. On coach's command to pull, the athlete grasps his right ankle and forces his helmet down to his right knee with steady force for a five second count. Without changing the position of his legs, the exerciser goes through the same pulling action only this time he tries to touch his helmet to his left knee, the knees are both still kept rigid and he must not bounce. To complete the exercise, the legs are reversed and the pulling action is performed on the leg over the helper's back first, then on the leg touching the ground.

2. The helper and the exerciser switch positions and the same

routine is followed. First the right leg is put up on the helper's back and the pull technique is done on the "up" leg and then on the "down" leg, each for a five count duration; the leg positions are then reversed and the process is repeated completing the entire cycle.

The Spine Stretching Exercise

1. The athlete kneels down on the ground; his toes should be flat on the ground, not dug in to the ground; his butt should be in between his heels and his arms folded across his shoulders.

2. From this starting position, the athlete will receive only one command from the coach, a signal to begin. The athlete must slowly lower his head back until he can touch his helmet to the ground. This action may be done several times, but should be done very slowly and gradually on a day-by-day basis until the athlete can go all the way down and touch his head to the ground with ease.

Coupled with the exercises described for the vital areas of the body, these more common areas of concern and the pull technique constitute what should be done every day. Once the athletes understand exactly how the exercises are to be performed, the time factor becomes minimal. Since practice time is valuable, many coaches have avoided going through a more thorough pre-practice or pre-game warmup than what they are accustomed to. Yet this routine in our practice session has never exceeded fifteen minutes, and the time spent can only be truly appreciated by those athletes who were never injured or who were able to withstand severe collisions without also sustaining severe injuries. Good organization before practice and games are the only ingredients necessary to make this exercise program payoff.

Index